IN SPECIAL NEED

A handbook for parents and young people in Scotland with special educational needs.

Prepared by **Graham Atherton**
Senior Research Officer,
Scottish Consumer Council

Scottish Consumer Council

Edinburgh
Her Majesty's Stationery Office

Scottish Consumer Council
314 St Vincent Street
Glasgow G3 8XW

© Crown Copyright 1989
First published 1989

Illustrations by 'Larry'

ISBN 0 11 493423 1

Contents

Preface

Since the publication of the Warnock report more than ten years ago, some major changes have taken place in our approach to the education of children and young people who, owing to some learning or other difficulty, such as physical disability, are believed to need help or support with their education beyond what is normally provided. Changes in the law — and increasingly, professional practice — have started to reflect a wider view of the "special educational needs" of these youngsters.

One important aspect of these changes is the increased recognition attached to the role of parents — above all parents of children with special needs — in not only providing encouragement and support at home but also in being adequately informed or consulted about key decisions affecting their children's education. The law now provides certain safeguards to ensure that parents are given an opportunity to become involved.

With this in mind, the Scottish Consumer Council (SCC) has prepared this handbook to guide parents and young people through the decision making processes, practices and issues they are likely to encounter in provision for special educational needs. It complements and expands on two other SCC publications, *The Law of the School*, about parents legal responsibilities and rights in a wide range of educational matters in Scotland, and *Keeping Parents Posted*, about arrangements and opportunities for providing parents in Scotland, England and Wales with written information about their children's schooling. Both of these are also published by HMSO Books.

Although some official and other public information for parents and young people with special educational needs has now become available — a development the SCC greatly welcomes — we have been made aware of the many parents and young people in Scotland who are without a detailed and comprehensive but readable guide to turn to in this area, either because nothing suitable is locally available or because they wish to deepen or broaden their understanding of the processes, practices or issues involved.

We believe that our handbook fills in these important gaps in public information for parents and young people in Scotland about provision for special educational needs. Our handbook will be of particular interest to parents of children whose difficulties are perhaps being assessed for the first time, to parents who want to know more about what can be done to help their child, and to parents and other people who wish to become more informed about some of the wider issues involved. Our handbook will also be of interest to parents' groups, school board members, local councillors, advice workers, teachers, specialist staff and all other people in contact with parents or children. It should also be of special use to people appointed as 'Named Person' to whom parents of children and young people with 'recorded' special educational needs can turn to for advice and information.

Having had to cope personally with a child with special educational needs, this handbook is of particular interest to me. I am only sorry it was not on the bookshelves much sooner. I am confident that parents and other readers will find this publication most informative. I commend it to you.

Barbara Kelly
Chairman
Scottish Consumer Council

Acknowledgements

The Scottish Consumer Council is particularly grateful to the following individuals for their helpful and detailed comments on drafts of the text.

Janet Cross, a parent and special school teacher; George Currie, St. Andrew's College of Education; Lady Mary Gray, principal educational psychologist, Strathclyde Regional Council; Peter Grainger, Scottish Curriculum Development Service and members of the Consultative Committee on the Curriculum's Committee on Special Educational Needs; John Hart, a parent and teacher; Jean Lawson, formerly of the Scottish Education Department, now retired; Frank McKee, senior educational psychologist, Strathclyde Regional Council; Leslie Meade, Association of Scottish Principal Educational Psychologists; Alastair Milne, HMI, Scottish Education Department; Gilbert MacKay, Jordanhill College of Education; Audrey Smith, Scottish Spina Bifida Association; Liz Sutherland, formerly of the Scottish Centre for the Tuition of the Disabled; Sylvia Sandeman, a parent and former member of the Scottish Consumer Council; Mr Ian Swanson, principal educational psychologist, Tayside Regional Council; Dr. George Thomson and colleagues, Department of Education, University of Edinburgh; Elizabeth Wallis, formerly of the Centre for Studies in Integration in Education; Adrian Ward, solicitor.

The SCC would like to thank education authorities for supplying copies of their information materials for parents of children and young people with special educational needs. The SCC is grateful to the many voluntary organisations which commented on particular sections in the text and to the Scottish Council on Disability for its assistance and support. Finally the SCC would like to thank the parents and the voluntary organisations who completed questionnaires about their satisfaction with and involvement in provision for special educational needs.

The reading list was compiled with the help of Elizabeth Wallis. Typescripts: Muriel Adam, Pearl Clark, Anne Shearer and Margaret Sloan.

Introduction

About one in five children and young people are estimated to require at some time additional or special help with their schooling because of some learning difficulty, social, emotional or medical problem, or physical disability or impairment. They are said to have "special educational needs".

The Warnock committee of enquiry, which reported over ten years ago, ushered in a new wave of thinking about the education of children and young people with special needs. One of its key recommendations was that children with some learning or other difficulty should not necessarily be educated apart from other children, for example, at a special school, but should as far as possible be educated alongside other children at ordinary or "mainstream" school.

The Warnock committee also attached great importance to the involvement of parents, as one of the main educators of their children, in the assessment and schooling of children with special educational needs. It suggested that information and advice should be made available to parents to enable them to play a meaningful part in professional decision making and understand fully what their children's special requirements are.

The law now gives parents, who have long been under a general legal duty to see that their children are properly educated, rights to be informed and consulted about the special educational needs of their child, including certain rights of appeal if they disagree with official decisions. The procedures involved are however fairly complicated and few parents have the legal knowledge or educational expertise to exercise their legal responsibilities and rights in this area as fully as they might.

This handbook has been written to fill this large gap in information and advice for parents of children and young people who have — or might have — special educational needs. Although some official information, books and other publications in this area are now available, not all of these are accessible, detailed or readable enough for parents to make much sense of their rights, responsibilities or role in provision for special educational needs.

This handbook is divided into five sections:

Part 1 explains the procedures which have to be followed in working out exactly what children's and young person's special educational needs are, with detailed guidance about how parents can become involved and what parents can do if they disagree with or are unhappy about what is, or is not, being done.

Part 2 briefly describes the range of specialist or extra help children and young people with various difficulties may require to be educated properly.

Part 3 covers the key issues and problems arising from provision for special educational needs which parents and groups of parents might want to take up with professional staff or their elected representatives.

Part 4 lists books and other publications which parents may wish to read to deepen and widen the knowledge and understanding of their children's difficulties or current policies and practices.

Part 5 gives the names, addresses and other details of national voluntary, educational and other organisations which can be turned to for further information, advice or practical help, including information about local contacts or groups.

The text attempts to explain complicated areas of law and complex issues in plain language as far as possible, but where the use of legal, official or technical terms is unavoidable these are explained in the text and in the list of key educational and legal terms at the end. Readers wanting information about the legal position of parents in areas of education outside the scope of this handbook are at appropriate points referred to another SCC publication: *The Law of the School*, published by HMSO Books, 1987. The SCC regrets that it cannot deal with enquiries or complaints from individuals.

Part One: Using the Law

What are special educational needs?

Children and young people* are said to have special educational needs, if compared with other children of similar age, they have much greater difficulties in coping with schooling and need some sort of extra help with their education. Traditionally children got help if they belonged to one or more of the several categories of "handicap", such as not being able to hear, see or learn properly. More often than not such children have attended special schools. About two per cent of children in Britain have been identified as needing such help.

Since the government committee of enquiry, the Warnock committee, reported some years ago, however, a wider view than this traditional one has been taken of the sorts of children and young people who may be described as having special educational needs. This wider view includes children with learning or other difficulties, which while not the most severe or complex ones schools have to deal with, nonetheless call for significant extra or specialist help. A great many of these children have mild learning or other difficulties which, while not calling for the sort of schooling for children with the most serious difficulties, nevertheless require some form of specialist support; frequently those children were to be found in what used to be called "remedial" classes at ordinary schools, but their difficulties, as often as not, could also go unnoticed. If this wider interpretation is adopted, as many as one in five children and young people are estimated to have special educational needs at some stage in their education, and one in six are estimated to be affected throughout their education. Most of these children attend ordinary schools, although in some cases they may be educated in special classes or units attached to ordinary schools.

An even broader view (but beyond the scope of this handbook) is that a very large proportion of children — perhaps more than half — have special educational needs. This proportion includes all those children who have difficulties with their schooling because of difficult home circumstances, because of their cultural or linguistic backgrounds, or because of inappropriate teaching. Children with special gifts or aptitudes — in art, music, science, practical skills, and so on — might

---

* Throughout the text "child" or "children" refers to anyone under school leaving age (age 16 approximately); young person refers to anyone over school age who has not reached 18. Unless otherwise indicated, for "child" or "children" read "young person" or "young persons" as well.

also be thought as having special educational needs which may not be sufficiently recognised or catered for by the educational system.

It is therefore not easy to give a straightforward answer to the question: what are special educational needs and what sort of children and young people are affected? Indeed, insofar, as every child is an unique individual, all children may have special educational needs of one sort or another, so the distinction between ordinary and special educational needs may be somewhat arbitrary. In many respects, whether or not a person has "special needs" is also relative to how well the education system is already geared up to catering for the whole range of individual differences: the more schools and other institutions adapt themselves to individuals' needs, the less likely are those needs to be regarded as "special". This may in turn be a reflection of the way in which the educational system is managed and resources (money, staff, equipment) are allocated.

This first part of this publication is concerned with showing how the law and the policies or practices of an education authority can be put to best possible use if there is reason to believe that a child has special educational needs, whether in the narrow or wider sense. Part two shows in more detail what sort of help can be given to deal with particular difficulties. Part three draws attention to some of the limitations of and problems in catering for special educational needs. We start off, however, by showing how thinking and provision in this area has developed, as this has an important bearing on later sections of the handbook.

How did education for children with special needs get started in Scotland?

In Scotland schooling for children requiring special help with their education (in its traditional sense) dates back to the setting up, by voluntary and private bodies, of such institutions as the Asylum for the Industrious Blind in Edinburgh in 1773, Donaldson's Hospital (now school) for the Deaf in Edinburgh in 1850, and establishments for the education of "imbeciles" and "defectives" at Dundee and Edinburgh in the middle of the nineteenth century. The education provided was largely limited to vocational training in manual skills for future employment. The Education (Scotland) Act 1872, which established a national system of public elementary education and made education compulsory between 5 and 13, did not include any separate provisions for special schooling. (Interestingly, though, within two years of the act, 50 blind children were known to have been receiving instruction in ordinary classes at Scottish schools — over a hundred years before the Warnock committee recommended an integrationalist approach to special schooling).

Special educational treatment

The first major attempt to introduce some sort of special provision into the public education system came with an act of 1906 covering special schooling for blind and deaf children. A later act of 1906 allowed school boards to provide special schooling for "epileptic, crippled and mentally handicapped children". Under another act of 1913, school boards had to "ascertain" which children in their area were mentally "defective", children being put into institutional care only if they were not considered capable enough to benefit from special schooling.

It was not until the Education (Scotland) Act of 1945, however, that education authorities, as part of their general duty to provide education according to age, ability and aptitude, had to ascertain which children in their area who had reached five had a disability of "mind or body" requiring "special educational treatment" at school (including occupational centres) and which of them were too handicapped to be suitable for education or training at school at all. To achieve this, authorities could require parents to submit their child for a medical examination (extended to a psychological examination after 1969); parents of children who had reached the age of two could also ask for an examination as well, the authority not being allowed to refuse their request without good reason. Parents could appeal to the Secretary of

State against a medical certificate which showed that their child required special educational treatment and to the sheriff court against being refused permission to withdraw their child from special school. Authorities were allowed (and, after 1969, required) to set up child guidance services, now renamed psychological services, to advise teachers and parents (and, from 1969, social work departments) about the education of children in difficulties and, if necessary, to provide special educational treatment. Authorities were also under a duty to make known the educational importance of "early ascertainment" of children with disabilities and opportunities for these children to be examined.

A series of advisory council reports on pupils suffering from physical or mental disabilities or from social or emotional "maladjustment" provided guidance for education authorities on the educational "treatment" of various difficulties children had. Regulations* issued in 1954 defined nine legal categories of "handicap" for which special educational provision should be made: deafness, partial deafness, blindness, partial sightedness, mental handicap, epilepsy, speech

---

* *Special Educational Treatment (Scotland) Regulations 1954*, Stat. instr. 1954/1239, as amended by S.I. 1956/894.

defects, maladjustment and physical handicap. The regulations did not, however, extend to the large number of those pupils with milder learning and other difficulties, or whose difficulties stemmed from such factors as absenteeism, or frequent change of school. The Schools (Scotland) Code 1956** laid down maximum class sizes for the various categories of handicap so as to ensure that pupils in special schools and classes got more individual attention.

It was clear, from a Scottish Education Department circular issued in 1955, that the "special educational treatment" envisaged was not officially regarded as a large scale system of separate "special schools" for children with a disability or handicap:

"It is recognised that there must continue to be situations where it is essential in children's interest that the handicapped must be separated from those who are not. Nevertheless as medical knowledge increases and as general school conditions improve it should be possible for an increasing proportion of pupils who require special educational treatment to be educated along with their contemporaries in ordinary schools. Special educational treatment should indeed be regarded simply as a well-defined arrangement within the ordinary educational system to provide for the handicapped child the individual attention that he particularly needs". *SED Circular 300, 1955* (para 4).

Special education

Between 1960 and 1970 four working parties were set up to consider what guidance could be given to education authorities on the ascertainment of mental handicap, maladjustment, auditory and visual handicap. Much of their thinking was brought to fruition in the Education (Scotland) Act of 1969, which did away with the concept of "special educational treatment", with its medical overtones and notion of fixed "disability of mind and body", in favour of a new one, "special education", defined as:

"… education by special means appropriate to the requirements of pupils whose physical, intellectual, constitutional or social development that cannot in the opinion of the education authority be adequately promoted by ordinary methods of education."

The act made it clear, in other words, that ascertainment was not a medical matter only, but also involved psychological, educational and

---

** S.I. 1956/894.

other reports as well, including, if possible, the views of the child's parents and teacher(s). The authority was also seen as initiating ascertainment from infancy, where appropriate, and not only from the age of five. The act, moreover, endorsed the growing view that ascertainment decisions were not final but required the education authority to keep regular watch over children's special education for a continuing period.

At the same time, there was increasing concern about the fate of children ascertained as being "uneducable and untrainable" and thus placed in local authority "day centres" or health authority mental hospitals. By 1973 a government working party concluded that no child was ineducable or untrainable, and this was given force in an act of 1974, under which care of severely and profoundly mentally handicapped children of school age was taken over by education authorities.

In spite of these developments, "special education" acquired a much narrower meaning than the law and official documents, like SED circular 300 (cited above), allowed for. Ascertainment came to be associated with children suffering from severe disabilities and handicaps (under two per cent of the school population) and with attendance at a special school. At the same time, the legal categories of handicap became increasingly hard to work with as realisation grew that there was not always any obvious link between a particular handicap and the sort of education a child required. A child with a serious physical handicap, such as paralysis of both legs, might not require special education at all, but simply specially adapted classrooms and equipment at an ordinary school. Conversely, a child with no physical or mental handicap but with a lot of emotional and social problems might require a lot of special attention and education beyond what is normally provided in the ordinary classroom. With advances in medicine, an increasing number of children were also surviving with "multiple handicaps" that did not fit readily into established categories.

Within the area of mental handicap, there was growing dissatisfaction with what counted as mild, moderate or severe learning difficulties, given the importance of other factors, such as support from the home, quality of tuition, type of cirricula etc. in influencing a child's progress at school. Indeed the distinction between children with handicaps and those without them appeared to have outlived its educational usefulness. It was with these issues in mind that the government appointed a committee of enquiry in 1974, chaired by Mary Warnock, to report on the education of handicapped children and young people.

What did the Warnock report say?

The Warnock report made a number of important recommendations which altered our way of thinking about special education and which resulted in certain changes in the law. The report coined the term "special educational need" to refer to a range of difficulties going beyond the old categories of handicap, which the report said should be abolished. It called for a change in the law to "embody a broader concept of special education related to a child's individual needs as distinct from his disability" and recommended that the distinction between special education and ordinary schooling should be abolished. While recognising a continuing need for special schools, the report suggested that children and young people with special needs should be educated in ordinary schools as far as possible — loosely referred to as "integration". It recommended a system of "recording" the needs of children with severe, complex or long-term disabilities, such as not being able to hear, speak, see, or move about properly. Recording should be carried out by multi-professional teams (teachers, psychologists, social workers, doctors, etc.) having regard to the needs of the whole child, not just those arising from specific disabilities. Children previously regarded as "mildly", "severely" or "profoundly mentally handicapped" were in future to be regarded as children with learning difficulties alongside children getting "remedial" help in ordinary schools.

The Warnock report therefore saw **special educational need** as applying not just to children with pronounced, specific or complex difficulties (representing about two per cent of the child population), but also to children and young people:

- whose difficulties were mainly emotional or social or who could be awkward or disruptive in class;

- in "remedial" classes whose difficulties stemmed from a variety of factors but who all too often were treated alike;

- whose difficulties were temporary or short-term, for example arising from frequent changes of or absences from school;

- whose difficulties resulted from the language in which they were taught being different from the language they spoke at home.

When these children and young people are added to those with the more obvious disabilities and handicaps, some twenty per cent or more children were estimated by the Warnock report to be in need of additional or special help with their education. The report also said that parents should be closely involved in the assessments of their child.

In its white paper "Special Educational Needs in Scotland" (1980), the government stated that it intended to introduce legislation reflecting "a single fundamental concept of special educational need which will comprehend not only those children who are at present in special schools and classes or receiving remedial education but also children with learning or other difficulties whose needs have hitherto lacked specific recognition".*

A progress report by the school inspectorate took what was probably an even wider view of special educational need, to cover children who have difficulty in coping with ideas and concepts as well as children with very basic learning difficulties.**

---

* Cmnd 7991, para. 5.
** Scottish Education Department, *The Education of Pupils with Learning Difficulties in Primary and Secondary Schools in Scotland: a progress report by HM Inspector of Schools*, HMSO, 1980.

What does the law now say?

The law now states that children and young people have special educational needs if they:

> have much greater difficulty in learning than most other children of their own age;

or

> suffer from a disability or handicap which prevents them being educated with their own age group;

or

> are under five years old and belong to either of these groups.

The law does not, however, cover children or young people who have problems with learning because they are taught in a language which is not the language they speak at home.

Duties of education authorities

Education authorities are under a general legal duty to secure adequate and efficient provision of school and further education in their areas, including adequate and efficient provision for children and young persons with special educational needs. Although the law does not define "adequate and efficient" education, this duty is understood to mean providing enough places at schools and further education colleges for people wanting them and providing a balanced, all-round curriculum (what is taught) according to the age, abilities and aptitudes of pupils and any special educational needs they have.

The law does not say that the education provided must, be "the best"; it merely states that it should not fall below what the court (in the last resort) deem adequate or efficient education. It is also difficult to take action through the courts to ensure that adequate and efficient education is in fact provided: in one court case brought by parents, the court ruled that the authority's provision of education could not be deemed less than adequate or efficient if circumstances, in this case teachers going on strike, made it impossible for the authority to carry out a statutory duty.*

---

* For further details, see under "Complaints" and "Legal Action" in the *Law of the School*, including provisions for making a formal complaint to the Secretary of State or going to the Court of Session if the education authority is thought to be failing in a legal duty.

In addition to their general duties, education authorities have certain specific responsibilities for securing adequate and efficient education for children and young persons with special educational needs:

- encouraging the "early discovery" of children with special needs, well before they are due to start school;

- finding out what children's special needs are by arranging for children to be expertly "assessed";

- recording, in a document known as the Record of Needs the difficulties and requirements of children and young people whose special needs are "pronounced", "specific" or "complex" and call for "continuing review" (see the list of "Key terms" at the end of the handbook for an explanation of these terms);

- appointing a Named Person for parents and young people to turn to for advice and information (except when they opt not to have one);

- setting up committees through which parents and young people can appeal against a recording decision or the content of the Record of Needs;

- keeping watch over a child's or young person's special needs and arranging for a formal review of these needs when necessary;

- reviewing the future needs of all recorded pupils between the ages of 14 and 15 years 3 months approximately.

Parents' responsibilities and rights

Parents are also under a general legal duty to ensure that their children from the age of five up to age sixteen, approximately, receive "efficient education", normally by seeing that they regularly attend school (but possibly by arranging for their children to be educated "by other means", for example, at home instead). The education provided must be suited to the age, ability and aptitude of the child and any special educational needs he or she has (whether these have been "recorded" or not).

In addition, the education authority must have regard to the principle that children should be educated in accordance with the wishes of their parents, provided that this does not interfere with the provision of efficient education or give rise to unreasonable public expenditure, such as having to employ extra staff or build extra classrooms. This principle applies to the sort of school parents would like their children to attend, such as an ordinary or a special school, but it applies to other aspects of education, too, such as what is taught. Bear in mind, though, that it is a principle which the authority must have "regard to"; the authority does not have to comply with parents wishes.

These important legal duties and rights are worth keeping in mind over and above the specific rights parents and young people have in provision for special educational needs.

If you think that the education authority is failing to carry out some legal duty properly or is not respecting your own legal duties or rights you can do a number of things:

- You could speak to the members of school or education authority staff concerned, including the psychological service to see if the matter can be resolved there and then, and if necessary, go to a higher authority — the director of education or the divisional education officer. You could also approach your regional or islands councillor to see what can be done;

- You could seek guidance from your Named Person (if you have one) or from a local advice centre, such as a citizens advice bureau, about whether you are on good legal grounds for taking further action against the authority;

- You could consult a solicitor. A local advice centre can put you in touch with solicitors dealing with your sort of case. Many solicitors belong to a scheme under which you are charged only £5 for the first half hour's worth of advice, regardless of your income; you may qualify for legal advice and assistance after that free of charge or at a reduced charge if your income is below a certain level (your local advice centre will again give you details).

Each of these sorts of people may be worth approaching without waiting until a situation has got out of hand and feelings are running high. Approaching a solicitor, for example, does not automatically mean that you must confront the education authority and threaten court action: this may simply end in deadlock and avoidable legal expense. A polite letter from the solicitor, pointing out the legal position, may be all that is necessary to put matters right, in a spirit of co-operation or negotiation. Disputes about speech therapy provision, for example, have been resolved satisfactorily in this way without taking the authority to court.

ASSESSMENT, RECORDING & REVIEW OF SPECIAL EDUCATIONAL NEEDS

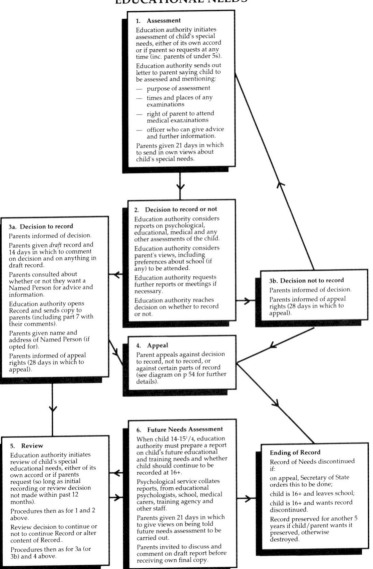

1. Assessment

Education authority initiates assessment of child's special needs, either of its own accord or if parent so requests at any time (inc. parents of under 5s).

Education authority sends out letter to parent saying child to be assessed and mentioning:

— purpose of assessment

— times and places of any examinations

— right of parent to attend medical examinations

— officer who can give advice and further information.

Parents given 21 days in which to send in own views about child's special needs.

2. Decision to record or not

Education authority considers reports on psychological, educational, medical and any other assessments of the child.

Education authority considers parent's views, including preferences about school (if any) to be attended.

Education authority requests further reports or meetings if necessary.

Education authority reaches decision on whether to record or not.

3a. Decision to record

Parents informed of decision.

Parents given *draft* record and 14 days in which to comment on decision and on anything in draft record.

Parents consulted about whether or not they want a Named Person for advice and information.

Education authority opens Record and sends copy to parents (including part 7 with their comments).

Parents given name and address of Named Person (if opted for).

Parents informed of appeal rights (28 days in which to appeal).

3b. Decision not to record

Parents informed of decision.

Parents informed of appeal rights (28 days in which to appeal).

4. Appeal

Parent appeals against decision to record, not to record, or against certain parts of record (see diagram on p 54 for further details).

5. Review

Education authority initiates review of child's special educational needs, either of its own accord or if parents request (so long as initial recording or review decision not made within past 12 months).

Procedures then as for 1 and 2 above.

Review decision to continue or not to continue Record or alter content of Record..

Procedures then as for 3a (or 3b) and 4 above.

6. Future Needs Assessment

When child 14-15¼, education authority must prepare a report on child's future educational and training needs and whether child should continue to be recorded at 16+.

Psychological service collates reports, from educational psychologists, school, medical carers, training agency and other staff.

Parents given 21 days in which to give views on being told future needs assessment to be carried out.

Parents invited to discuss and comment on draft report before receiving own final copy.

Ending of Record

Record of Needs discontinued if:

on appeal, Secretary of State orders this to be done;

child is 16+ and leaves school;

child is 16+ and wants record discontinued.

Record preserved for another 5 years if child/parent wants it preserved, otherwise destroyed.

Note: References to parent also normally apply to young persons.

Assessment: how are a child's special educational needs worked out?

The process of finding out what your child's special educational needs are and what should be done about them is called "assessment". The purpose of assessment is to find out whether your child's difficulties are such that they need to be officially recorded (in a document called the Record of Needs — see pages 41 to 47 below) and kept close watch over. Only difficulties regarded as "pronounced", "severe" or "complex" will be recorded. Assessment begins with the awareness or discovery that your child has difficulties in coping with ordinary everyday matters compared with other children, such as not hearing or seeing properly. These difficulties may have been discovered at or soon after birth, but it is possible in other cases that you or others dealing with your child have not become aware of any difficulties until much later on, perhaps not until your child has started school. Assessment is best regarded as a process involving observation of your child over a period of time, perhaps lasting several months, and not a short one-off exercise.

If you or the education authority think that your child has difficulties likely to call for a good deal of extra help with his or her education, a formal assessment will be carried out. The authority can arrange for your child to be assessed at any age, but the authority must do so as soon as your child has reached five if it thinks your child's difficulties are likely to require "recording" (see below). You yourself can also ask for an assessment; you simply write to the authority requesting an assessment. Although you need not give reasons for your request, it will probably help all concerned if you do so. Your request may not be turned down without good reason.

The assessment of your child must include educational, psychological and medical assessments, but assessments by social workers or other experts may be involved as well. The educational assessments may include reports from children's teachers, but these are not obligatory. The assessment must also take into account the views of the parents. The views of your child may be considered as well, but there is a legal obligation to do so only if he or she is 16 or over and is deemed capable of expressing his or her views. You are legally entitled to be present at any medical examinations connected with the assessment of your child, and the education authority must inform you of your right to be there when writing to you about this. The authority is not, however, under any statutory duty to let you attend any of the assessments, and it may be impracticable for you to do so if these take place over a period of time. The authority may nonetheless agree to let you attend or take part in any discussions at the end of the assessment process.

How soon should assessment be carried out?

The Warnock report emphasised how essential it was for a child's education that any special needs he or she has should be discovered and assessed as soon as possible. Education authorities must promote the importance of early discovery and opportunities for early assessment of special educational needs. The law does not say how this should be done but education authorities should be expected to encourage medical staff (doctors, health visitors) or social workers to alert them to children likely to have difficulties with their education. Authorities could also arrange for parents and other people, such as voluntary workers, to receive advice or information about the importance of early discovery and opportunities for children to be assessed. Severe difficulties like physical disability are likely to be discovered at birth or early in infancy, but the difficulties of many children may not become apparent until they have started school, for example, difficulties in concentrating or with eye-to-hand co-ordination while learning to read or write.

There are various ways you as a parent can help to make sure that any difficulties your child might have are acted upon:

- Spend time with your child, watch him or her play, listen and talk to your child, note your child's reactions to his or her surroundings. Bear in mind, though, that children do develop (or learn to talk, read, etc.) at different rates, and that something which at first sight might appear to be a difficulty may go away as your child gets older. Speak to your doctor or health visitor about anything regarding your child which is causing you concern. At the same time, avoid letting your worries spill over onto your child as this might only create more difficulties.

- Make an appointment with the psychological service of the education authority, which may arrange for your child to be assessed. Feel free to express any anxieties you might have. Do not hesitate to ask for an assessment yourself — this is your right — if you have any lingering doubts.

- Speak about any difficulties to others in regular contact with your child, such as playgroup or nursery school staff and social workers.

- If your child is identified as having particular difficulties, get in touch with any voluntary organisations concerned with those difficulties for further advice and information about what can be done to help your child. Your local advice centre should be able to give you their names and addresses. The national voluntary organisations listed at the end of this handbook can also put you in touch with any local branches in your area.

If you think that your concerns are not being listened to properly or taken seriously, you should, as already suggested above, voice them at a higher level, for example by writing to the director of education for your area, or, if necessary, complaining to your local councillor or MP or consulting a solicitor.

Before your child is due to be formally assessed

You will get a letter from the education authority saying that your child is to be formally assessed. (This letter may be delivered to you personally and/or with a note of explanation about what is involved). In practice, you may have already been contacted by staff informally before you hear from the authority officially; staff will probably want to talk to you about your child before the formal assessment begins.

You will be given the name of a contact person in the education department, a psychologist or education official, who can give you more information and advice. This person is responsible for making sure that your wishes, particularly concerning the school you want your child to go to, are passed on to the education authority. He or she should not be confused with the 'Named Person' (see pages 49 to 51), who is not appointed until later on.

You will be given at least 21 days in which to send in your own views, which will be considered during the assessment. The assessment itself may span a period of weeks or months; there are no legal limits on the time in which assessments must be completed.

Young persons (aged sixteen-seventeen) can also ask for an assessment at any time as long as they are still receiving school education. They cannot be assessed against their will, however. In some cases they may not be able to express themselves at all, and parents are entitled to ask for an assessment instead. In any event, you are still in a position to advise your child and make your views known to the education authority, no matter what the young person's state of mind may be. The authority is allowed to decide what sort of assessment to carry out, but otherwise the procedures are as for children of school age.

What sort of things may those assessing your child have to consider?

Those assessing your child will first want to identify what your child's strengths and weaknesses are. They will then go on to identify specific impairments or difficulties your child has and how these affect his or her education. Only after these things have been done will they work out your child's specific requirements and how his or her needs should be met, in terms of the following sorts of questions:

- Do your child's difficulties call for a different or modified curriculum from what is normally taught at school, for example, a curriculum suited to the needs of very slow learners?

- Does your child require specialist tuition and other support (e.g. specialist adaptations) to help with learning, for example, tuition in sign language or provision of books with special print?

- Does your child require therapeutic support to develop certain skills or carry out various tasks, for example, speech therapy or physiotherapy?

- Does your child need additional emotional and social support to cope with schooling, for example through more individual attention and tuition in smaller classes?

- Does your child require auxiliary help with everyday practical tasks, such as operating equipment, eating, toileting and so on?

A major question may be whether your child should be placed in an ordinary or special school if he or she requires a lot of specialist help. This question is considered in more detail on pages 35 to 40 and 123 to 128.

How should parents be involved in the assessment?

When your child is being assessed, you should expect:

- *to be as closely involved as possible and regarded as an "equal partner" with the experts and officials assessing your child.* Although this is not a legal requirement, it is a hallmark of good practice and is recommended in the government's guidance note to education authorities. It means that you should be given a chance to meet and discuss your child's difficulties with the people assessing your child. These people who should let you know what their own views are and what advice they will be passing on to the education authority. You should complain to the director of education of your authority if you think that you have not been properly involved or consulted, reminding the authority of the government guidance on this matter. You could ask to see copies of any background reports on your child prepared by those assessing your child — this could be important if you decide to appeal — although these documents need not be shown to you.

- *the assessment to be as wide-ranging as possible, involving not only doctors and psychologists but also other experts with specific knowledge of your child's difficulties.* This might, for example, include assessments by specialist teachers, social workers, or health visitors. You could also arrange expert assessments of your own. Voluntary organisations concerned with your child's difficulties may be able to provide expert advice or help to put you in touch with somebody who can.

- *the assessment to form part of a continuing process of keeping watch over your child's difficulties, throughout schooling if necessary.* The education authority must keep your child's special educational needs under regular review. It can do this by arranging for the school to keep special watch over your child's progress and to report to you and the authority each year. You should expect to receive a written report on your child's progress at least once a year and be given a chance to discuss this with school staff. You could also ask to see the official progress record which must be kept on your child, although the school is not obliged to let you see this* . Schools will normally give you every encouragement to meet staff and perhaps let you watch your child at work.

The education authority may also conduct a formal review of its own when it thinks necessary or when parents request the authority to do so (see pages 59 to 60). This will happen if it is thought that your child, if recorded, no longer has special educational needs or if these needs have changed in some way. A formal review may not, however, take place more than once every 12 months. An assessment of your child's "future needs" must also be carried out before your child reaches school leaving age (see pages 61 to 64).

Practical ways parents can help

There are a number of ways in which you can help those carrying out the assessment to work out what is best for your child:

- *You could provide your own observations or assessments of your child's difficulties.* It may be worthwhile keeping a diary to write these down in. You might want to note down such things as:

    how attentive, inquisitive or imaginative your child is;

    how your child spends his or her time;

    how self-reliant your child is in coping with ordinary everyday tasks.

    Note down your child's *strong* points, not just weak ones.

- *You could describe the amount of support and encouragement your child can get at home.* Here you could draw attention to:

    the amount of time you and your family (including brothers and sisters) are able to devote to your child, through recreational and other activities.

    The effects — positive and negative — your child's difficulties may be having on other members of your family, particularly on any brothers and sisters. Conversely, you could point to any problems or difficulties faced by other members of your family and the

---

* For further details, see under "School reports and records" in *The Law of the School*. The progress record is an official folder or file of information about your child, containing educational, medical, psychological and other details. It is possible that the law may be changed in the near future to let you see the progress record. The progress record should not be confused with the Record of Need (see pages 41 to 47 below) or the "school report" on your child normally sent to you each year.

effects they might be having on your child, for example, arising from chronic illness or marital breakdown.

any special facilities or adaptations for your child at home — for example, to help with mobility.

You should expect to be given every encouragement and opportunity to put your point of view across to those assessing your child. You will get another chance to express your views, in writing, should a decision be made to "record" your child (see below). You may find it worthwhile approaching one of the voluntary organisations concerned with your child's difficulties (mentioned at the end of this handbook) for help and advice in putting across your point of view.

After the assessment

After the assessment, the education authority will have to decide whether your child's difficulties are:

- "pronounced", "specific" or "complex" as to call for the opening of an official document, known as the Record of Needs, saying what your child's special requirements are (see pages 41 to 47);

- not so "pronounced", "specific" or "complex" as to require the opening of a Record of Needs but which nonetheless call for the provision of extra or special facilities or support for your child: for example, adaptations to school buildings, equipment or extra tuition;

- not ones which require specialist or additional support at all.

Before it can decide whether a Record of Needs should be opened, the authority must consider:

- reports from those assessing your child, including reports by medical and psychological staff and any social work or other reports on your child (including reports on any assessments you have arranged privately);

- the reports or other information from the school (if any) your child has attended;

- your own views about your child's special needs and the school you would like your child to attend;

- whether the school that the authority recommends that your child should attend is in fact suitable, for example, in terms of class size, tuition, adaptations, facilities or other support services available there.

The authority may invite you to take part in a "case conference" discussion at the end of the assessment process, though it is not legally obliged to. At this, reports and assessments on your child will be discussed and you may be encouraged to express your own views. You may be allowed to bring along a friend or somebody else who could help you to put across your point of view.

After all reports and your own views have been considered, the education authority must let you know in writing whether it has decided to draw up a Record of Needs for your child, giving the reasons for its decision. It must also give you information about your appeal rights (see pages 53-58).

Which school?

The most important decision parents and education authorities are likely to face is selecting a school which best meets a child's special educational needs. Depending on what your child's difficulties are, you and the authority may have to consider whether your child should attend an ordinary school, or whether your child would, in fact, be better off in a special school (or in a special class or unit attached to an ordinary school). You should expect to receive as much expert guidance as possible about this, but you should not hesitate to make your own views, preferences and disagreements known and taken notice of. You may, for example, have good reasons for wanting your child to be taught alongside children at ordinary school rather than in a special school. But, equally, you may believe that your child should be educated at a special school. It is not a purpose of this handbook to say whether your child should attend an ordinary or a special school. However, the handbook suggests below and later on (on pages 123 to 128) some of the points you may want to put to the education authority in support of your preference.

The decision about which school (if any) your child should go to will be worked out with you at the assessment stage. It is likely to be influenced by the following considerations:

- the nature of your child's difficulties and requirements;

- the social and emotional needs of your child;

- the availability of specialist services or facilities;

- your own preferences.

A careful balance may have to be struck between these considerations, although, in the final analysis, some considerations may end up carrying more weight than others.

Legal rights

The law* gives you a certain amount of say about which school your child should go to:

---

* For more detailed information, see the section on "choice of school," in *The Law of the School*, pp 50-60.

- In carrying out any of its functions, the education authority is under a general legal duty to "have regard" to the principle that children are to be educated according to the wishes of their parents, provided that this does not result in your child receiving unsuitable education or in unreasonable public expenditure, such as having to employ extra staff.

- The education authority must pay careful attention to your preferences about the school you would like your child to go to when carrying out any formal assessments and reviews of your child's special educational needs.

- The education authority must give you a chance to make a "placing request" for another school whenever it offers your child a place at a school it has selected for you. This should happen before your child is due to start school for the first time or is due to be transferred to another school, but you can make a placing request at any other time as well.

- You can appeal to an appeal committee against the refusal of a placing request or (where applicable) against the school named in your child's Record of Needs (see pages 41-47). You have a further right of appeal to the sheriff court against this aspect of your appeal. Your appeal may have to be considered by the Secretary of State before the committee or the court can decide whether to grant the school of your choice. The Secretary of State's advisers will want to hear your views, not just those of the education authority, about the school you would like your child to attend.

- You may be able to send your child to an independent school catering for your child's special needs. A number of these schools exist in Scotland, and the education authority may agree to pay for your child's education at one if it has no suitable school of its own. The authority need not do so, however, if it can show, should you appeal (see pages 52-58), that it can provide suitable education at less cost at one of its own schools and it has offered your child a place there. However it must arrange for your child to attend an independent school catering for your child's needs if ordered to by an appeal committee or the court.**

** In one court case, the sheriff ruled that the education authority was also obliged to send a child to an appropriate school outwith Scotland if there was not a suitable school in Scotland, but that ruling was reversed by the sheriff principal on appeal by the education authority.

Working out your choice of school

Should you decide to make a placing request or appeal, you do not have to give any reasons for wanting to send your child to one school rather than another, although it may help all concerned if you do so. Among the considerations you are likely to have in mind, with particular regard to your child's difficulties, when choosing a school are:

- Is your child likely to be happy and well cared for at a particular school? Will his or her difficulties be appreciated or understood by fellow pupils and staff? Are staff there friendly and approachable?

- Does the school's approach to learning or the way the school is organised (e.g. timetabling) fit in with your child's requirements?

- Does the school have the facilities and staffing your child requires? Even if it does not, it may be possible to get things changed when discussing your choice of school at the assessment stage. Education authority staff may then recommend that the help or support your child requires should be provided at the school of your choice.

- Is the school convenient to reach by ordinary transport? Can special transport, including paid attendants, be provided? (The education authority will normally meet the costs of any special transport required). How much travelling time is likely to be involved?

Other considerations might include whether any brothers, sisters or friends of your child attend the school, the school's extra curricular activities, and so on.

Grounds for refusing you your choice of school

The education authority, the appeal committee, or the court can turn down your request or appeal for a place at a particular school only on one or more of the following legally permitted grounds. It must have considered your child's special needs very carefully before doing so. It may turn down your request if letting your child attend the school of your choice would result in:

- the authority having to take an additional teacher into employment. The authority may, however, transfer a teacher from another school or provide a peripatetic (visiting) teacher to meet your child's needs at the school of your choice.

- the authority having to spend a lot of money altering or extending the school, such as building an extra classroom. What counts as a lot of money would, of course, be for the appeal committee or the court to decide on, but it is unlikely that the authority would be justified in refusing your request if only minor alterations or adaptations were involved, such as installing ramps or widening entrances.

- serious interference with the continuity of your child's education. If your child has already had several changes of the school, the authority might be justified in refusing yet another change.

- serious interference with order and discipline at the school and the well-being of pupils there. The authority might be able to argue that the school you want is not able to cater for your child's special needs without this causing disruption in class, for example, if your child requires a lot of individual attention or supervision that the school is unable to provide. It would be up to the authority to prove that this was the case before the appeal committee or the court could be satisfied that refusal of your placing request was justified.

The authority, appeal committee or court can also turn down your request or appeal if the school you want your child to go to:

- is a single sex school and does not normally admit children of your child's sex.

- is not suited to the age, ability or aptitude of your child. All ordinary schools are meant to cater for a broad range of ability, but the authority could argue that your child's learning difficulties are such as to call for a special school.

- is a special school and your child does not have special educational needs which are normally catered for there. A special school is a school catering wholly or mainly for children with a Record of

Needs, so that if your child is not already recorded (or likely to be) it is less likely that he or she will be offered a place there.

- is a school from which your child has already been excluded, for example, as a result of misbehaviour there.*

The education authority can nevertheless make an exception to those grounds for refusal, as indeed may the appeal committee or the court, which may decide that the circumstances of your child's case are exceptional enough to justify sending him or her to the school you want. The appeal committee or the court must, in any case, be satisfied that the authority was "in all the circumstances" justified in turning down your placing request, otherwise it must grant your request.

As explained on pages 52-58, the appeal committee (or the court) may have to refer your appeal to the Secretary of State before deciding whether to grant you the school of your choice: this will certainly happen where you and the authority hold different views about the nature and extent of your child's needs.

Before deciding which school you want your child to go to:

- Refer to pages 35-40 to consider whether you would prefer your child to be educated in an ordinary or a special school or in some other way (for example, in a special class at an ordinary school).

- Speak to teachers, the psychological service and other professional staff about your child's difficulties and the type of schooling most suitable for your child. Your Named Person (if you have one, or if you know who this is likely to be) may also agree to advise you.

- Collect as much information as you can about the school you are interested in sending your child to (the education authority must provide you with written information, normally in school handbooks, about any of the schools you ask about). Arrange visits to those schools, get staff to show you around and let you see for yourself what special adaptations, facilities and other help it can or *could* provide. (See part 2 of this handbook about the sort of special help or support which may be provided).

Do not necessarily expect to find a school in your area exactly suited to your child's special needs. It may be that your child's needs can only be catered for at a special school some distance away (in very exceptional

---

* For more detailed information about "exclusion from school", see *The Law of the School*, pp 100-104.

cases, your child may have to be educated at home or in hospital). At the same time, do not assume that because specialist help is not currently provided in the schools you are interested in, you must accept a school elsewhere. The Record of Needs will identify the kind of specialist help required and the education authority may be able to arrange to provide this at the school you want your child to go.

Appealing against the refusal of a placing request

You should be consulted about which school to send your child to during the assessment process, but if you and the authority cannot agree and your placing request has been turned down, you can appeal. You simply write to the committee saying that you want to appeal. The education authority will tell you who to write to. You need not give any reasons for your appeal, although it will probably help all concerned if you do so. You can appeal against sending your child to an ordinary or a special school.*

The committee may turn down your appeal only on one or more of the grounds mentioned above. If, however, your appeal is also related to the recording of your child, then the appeal will have to be referred to the Secretary of State (see pages 56-58). The committee must then decide, in the light of the Secretary of State's decision, whether the education authority is justified in turning down your placing request on one or more of the grounds described above. For example, if the school named in the Record is a special school and you want your child to go to an ordinary school, the appeal committee may then be in a position to grant your choice should the Secretary of State order the Record to be discontinued or order certain changes to be made in Record.

---

* For more information about appeal committee procedures, see *The Law of the School*, pp 55-60 and pp 215-219.

How are special educational needs recorded?

Once your child has been assessed, the authority has to decide whether he or she has difficulties and special needs which are "complex", "severe" or "specific" enough as to require recording in a document called the "Record of Needs" (see list of key terms at the end of the handbook for an explanation of each of these terms). This document says what your child's difficulties — and strengths — are, what additional or special help your child needs, how the education authority proposes to help, and other details, including the school to be attended.

The authority might, for example, decide that your child has hearing, learning, mobility or other difficulties which call for special tuition, adaptations, therapy and so on. It will then have to draw up a Record of Needs giving these and other details. After your child has been assessed, the authority must therefore:

- let you know in writing whether or not it has decided to record your child and give you the reasons why.

- show you a draft of what it proposes to enter in the Record of Needs (this may be delivered to you personally).

- give you 14 days in which to comment on its decision and on the drafted contents of the Record (your comments will be recorded in the Record). The contact person appointed by the authority to give you information and advice should be able to help you with this. You could also approach your Named Person (see pages 49-51) for help if you know who this is likely to be.

After considering any views you might have expressed, the authority must then give you a finalised version of the Record of Needs, together with:

- written information about your rights of appeal. You can appeal against the authority's decision to record and against certain parts of the Record (see section pages 52-58). You also have, since June 1987, a right of appeal against a decision *not* to record.

- the name and address of the Named Person, unless you have decided not to have a Named Person. The Named Person is somebody, such as a professional worker or close friend, to whom you can turn for advice and information about your child's special educational needs and who may be able to help you in future dealings with the education authority: for example, if you decide to appeal or when your child's special educational needs are brought under review.

What exactly does the Record of Needs say?

The Record of Needs is an official document describing what your child's special needs are, what additional help is required by your child to take advantage of education, and how the education authority proposes to cater for your child's special needs. This record can only be opened if your child's special educational needs are "pronounced", "specific" or "complex" and require to be kept continuing watch over. In an attempt to get away from the old categories of handicap, the law does not say exactly what sorts of difficulties should be recorded; in all cases it will be the nature and extent of the need which should determine the decision to record or not, although, in practice, all the former categories of handicap (see page 16) are likely, to be recorded.

The record has nine parts and includes information about your child's abilities and disabilities, what is required for his/her education, what the education authority proposes to do, your own views, and details about reviews of your child's needs.

Parts 1 and 2

Your child's name, address, sex and date of birth.
Your own name and address.
Name and address of the Named Person (except if you have chosen not to have a Named Person). This is the person parents of recorded children can turn to for advice and information (see pages 49-51). You cannot appeal against the choice of Named Person in the Record, that is, for a choice of a Named Person who is more acceptable to you. (This should not, of course, arise if you have been properly consulted about the choice of Named Person in the first place).

Part 3

(a) A description of your child. This covers your child's health, ability, interests, emotional development, and how well your child can talk, see and hear. It also describes educational attainment of your child, if at school. You cannot appeal against this part of the Record.

(b) A description of your child's difficulties or disabilities and the sort of specialist help needed. This is called a "summary of impairments". You can appeal against this part of the record.

You should expect all of part 3 of the Record, and indeed the rest of the Record, be written in plain language, avoiding technical terms you cannot be expected to understand.

Part 4

This part, the "statement of special educational needs", says in more detail what your child's requirements are for his or her proper educational development, such as the provision of a modified curriculum, specialist tuition or learning in small groups, therapeutic support, and so on. You can appeal against this part of the record.

Part 5

This part tells you what special measures to help your child are proposed (a) by the education authority and (b) by the providers of other services, for example, the health board or social work department. You cannot appeal against this part of the Record.

Part 6

The name of the school to be attended. A school will not be named of course if your child is too young to go to school or is to be educated at home. You can appeal against this part of the record (but only if your placing request for a school of your own choice has already been turned down by the authority).

Part 7

The views of the "responsible party" — this will usually be yourself as parent but could refer to a child's guardian or the person having custody of or liable to maintain the child, such as a foster parent. In this part of the Record you can disagree with any part of the record, including the parts you cannot appeal against, such as part 5, about how the authority proposes to help your child. Expressing your disagreement here does not initiate an appeal however — this has to be done separately.

Part 8

This section contains details of any further assessments carried out, decisions about whether to continue the Record after review, and changes to the content of the Record. You must be given the chance to comment on any changes before they are entered in the Record. Earlier entries remain in the Record after review so that those reading the Record can see what successive measures have been adopted.

Part 9

This contains the names of people who have been given a copy or copied extracts of the Record, such as medical staff. It also mentions the names of officials who supplied these copies and the dates when the information was given out, returned or destroyed. It need not list the names of people who have simply been allowed to see the Record but not supplied with their own copy.

You must be told about any changes that are made to the Record, and your own copy must be brought up to date. If you move to another area, your child's Record must be transferred to the education authority in that area — this authority then becomes responsible for your child's special needs. If your child is being educated outside Scotland, your permission is needed before a copy of the Record can be sent there, however.

Making your views known about the Record of Needs

As mentioned above, you will be asked in a letter from the authority to comment on the decision to record your child and on the content of the Record of Needs itself. The authority may send you a *draft* of the actual Record it proposes to open, or it may simply show you what information it proposes to enter in the Record without showing you the actual document itself. Your views should already have been taken into account by the authority in reaching its decision and drawing up the Record. Your written comments on the recording decision and the Record itself will appear in the space provided in part 7 of the Record in its final form.

Before making any comments

- ask the education authority, if necesssary, for a proper explanation of its decision to record or what proposed entries for the Record mean, especially if you think that your views have been ignored or if there are entries or statements you do not understand. The official appointed to give you advice and information (not to be confused with the Named Person, who is appointed later on) should be able to give you help here, or put you in touch with somebody else who can help you.

- ask for whatever additional advice or guidance you can get from those professionally involved with your child, such as doctors, teachers, social workers and psychologists. You may want to do this if you still feel uncertain, after the Record has been drawn up, about what is best for your child. The person likely to be appointed as your

Named Person, if you have opted to have one, may also agree to advise you if approached.

- Then study the entry for each part of the Record carefully, asking yourself such questions as:

  Do you want to have a Named Person at all? (You are not legally obliged to have one). Is the Named Person, if mentioned in *part 2*, somebody really acceptable to you? Is he or she somebody you feel is approachable, trustworthy and reliable? (This should not, of course, be a problem if, as usually happens, you have been invited to nominate somebody yourself.)

  Does *part 3*, of the Record give an accurate or fair picture of what your child's difficulties are? Have some difficulties been missed out or glossed over? Are some difficulties overstated, for example, behaviour problems?

  Does it also say enough *positive* things about your child, saying what your child *can* do and not just what he or she cannot do?

  Does *part 4* of the Record give a precise or detailed enough picture of what your child's requirements are? Does it, for example, describe properly what the specialist tuition or therapy, is meant to achieve.

  Is *part 5* of the record, what the authority proposes to do, in your view, consistent with the description of your child's difficulties and requirements in parts 3 and 4 of the Record? Although you cannot *appeal* against this part of the Record, you are still entitled to express your disagreement with it (your views are entered in part 7 of the Record). You should get outside expert advice if necessary, for example from a voluntary organisation or sympathetic specialist, if you feel at all doubtful about the help the authority proposes to offer.

  Does *part 6* represent your own choice of school? Is the school proposed the right *sort* of school for your child, whether an ordinary or a special school? Are you convinced that the school can offer the right kind of support, tuition, and so on? Will it be convenient enough to reach? Can you imagine your child settling down and feeling happy there?

  Part 7 is reserved specially for your comments. If you have difficulty putting your views down, perhaps you could get a trusted friend or adviser to help you (this could be your Named Person if he or she is willing to act on an informal basis until being officially appointed).

Parts 8 and 9 deal with administrative matters only, so you need not comment on these parts of the Record.

Keep your own copy of the draft content of the Record sent to you for comment. You can compare these statements with what is put in the copy of the finalised Record. This could be important should you decide to appeal.

Who is allowed to see the Record of Needs?

The education authority keeps the original document and has to give you a copy. Another copy is kept at your child's school (if applicable). The Record is a confidential document and can only be shown to:

- the person appointed to advise you (the Named Person).

- the government official dealing with your case, should your appeal go to the Secretary of State.

- the Reporter, should your child be referred to a children's hearing.

These people must be supplied with a copy if they ask for one. The authority may also show the Record (except part 7 with your comments) to teachers, psychologists, medical staff and social workers dealing with your child. It can also be shown to research workers. These people must have good reasons for wanting to see it. The Record cannot normally be shown to anyone else except with your written permission.

Discontinuing the Record of Needs

A record must be "discontinued" by the education authority as a result of:

- an appeal or review decision to discontinue it.

- your child leaving school.

- your child asking for it to be discontinued if he or she is over school leaving age (age 16 approx).

- You as parent asking for the record to be discontinued if, in the education authority's view, your child, being over school age, is deemed not to be in a position to make such a request.

The education authority must normally keep the "discontinued" Record for another five years. The record must then be destroyed and you — or your child if over school age — must be told that this has been done. If the Record has been discontinued as a result of a decision by the Secretary of State, the authority must destroy it straightaway, unless you ask it not to do so. You must be given 21 days after being told that the Record has been discontinued to say whether you want the record preserved. If you do, the Record will be kept for another five years; otherwise it will be destroyed.

What does the Named Person Do?

One of the key recommendations of the Warnock report was that parents of children and young people with (or showing signs of having) special educational needs should have a single point of contact, the Named Person, to turn to for advice, information and support. Warnock suggested that, for children who had not started school, the Named Person could be a health visitor, and for children who had started school, the child's headteacher, who is normally the first point of contact for parents about educational matters.

The law, while not carrying out the Warnock recommendations in full, now gives parents and young persons the right to turn to a Named Person for advice and information. This provision is limited, however, to those with a *Record of Needs*, not to parents of children and young people with special educational needs which have gone *unrecorded* (and who account for about another 18 per cent of those at school).

The Named Person is appointed at the same time as the Record of Needs is opened (and *not* as soon as it appears a child has special educational needs). You must first, however, be allowed to say whether you in fact want a Named Person (until June 1987 the authority had to appoint a Named Person for each recorded child, whether the parent wanted one or not); you may prefer to manage without a Named Person to turn to. If you agree to have a Named Person, the authority will then appoint somebody, perhaps inviting you to make your own nomination, although the authority need not accept your nomination. (The education authority may agree to the Named Person becoming involved before being officially appointed, while your child is still being assessed, if it looks likely that your child will be recorded.)

Who can be appointed?

Although the law does not say who should be appointed as the Named Person, he or she should be somebody you can trust and rely upon and who has some understanding of your child's difficulties and needs. This could be somebody already involved in education, such as a headteacher or psychologist, but equally the person could be somebody such as a doctor, minister, voluntary worker, or close friend. One advantage of having a Named Person employed in education, such as a specialist teacher, for example, is that he or she may have expert knowledge which can be brought to bear on your child's difficulties or requirements. A major disadvantage is that he or she might not be in a position to give you the support you need should a conflict or dispute arise between yourself and the education authority. A Named Person not employed by the education authority may feel more committed to giving you support. The National Bureau for Handicapped Children has produced a helpful guide about choosing a Named Person.*

Responsibilities of the Named Person

The Named Person does not have any strict legal duties. Government guidance to education authorities indicates that the Named Person should give advice and information to parents about appealing against a recording decision or asking for a formal review of their child's special educational needs. The Named Person may also agree to accompany you or speak on your behalf at appeals, reviews, future needs assessments, or other dealings with the education authority, but is not obliged to do so (nor need he or she be informed that any of these things are taking place). The Named Person should not necessarily be

---

* Philippa Russell, "The Role of the Named Person", National Bureau for Handicapped Children.

regarded as your *legal representative* — you will probably need a solicitor to represent you at appeals.

Although the Named Person need not be given any formal training, he or she is expected to have some basic knowledge of the workings of the educational system, including provisions for assessing and recording special educational needs. Education authorities are relied on to provide any formal training, and at least one college of education in Scotland (Jordanhill) is known to run its own course for Named Persons.

You should expect the Named Person to be easy to get in touch with or see you at reasonable times (write or phone for an appointment) and be willing to spend enough time with you. He or she should also be able to deal confidently with officials and specialist staff and provide you with support. This does not mean that the Named Person has to agree with your point of view, merely that he should help you to put your views across and perhaps alert you to any differences of viewpoint between yourself and professional staff.

You can ask for a change of Named Person at any time. This might arise as your child moves from primary to secondary school or approaches school leaving age, or if for any reason you become unhappy with the person appointed. Simply write to the director of education for your authority, asking for somebody else acceptable to you to be appointed.**

** For further details, see *Information for the Named Person*, Scottish Society for the Mentally Handicapped.

How can you appeal against a recording decision?

If you disagree with a recording decision or with something in parts 3b, 4 or 6 of the Record (see pages 41-47), it may be possible to get matters changed by making an appeal. If you have been properly involved in the assessment and recording processes, disagreement and the wish to appeal is not likely to arise. Should disagreement occur, however, it is important to be clear about what your appeal rights are and what you are appealing against, to save time and possible frustration later on.

Your Named Person (if you have one) should give you advice and guidance about appealing. You may also want to consult a solicitor as well; many solicitors belong to a scheme in which they offer advice at a charge of only £5 for the first half hour. You may also qualify for further advice and assistance free of charge or at reduced cost, depending on your income (this does not cover the cost of legal representation at appeal hearings; separate *legal aid* may be available for this should your case go to court). Remember, using a solicitor need not commit you into making an appeal; it may be that a polite letter from your solicitor to the education authority pointing out your legal position may be all that is necessary to put matters right.

What can you appeal against?

You can appeal against:

- a decision to open or (after review) continue a Record of Needs.

- (since June 1987) a decision *not* to open or continue a Record of Needs.

- statement *part 3b* of the Record of Needs summarising your child's impairments or difficulties.

- statements in *part 4* of the Record saying what your child's requirements are in order to be educated properly.

- *part 6* of the Record naming the school (if any) proposed by the education authority.

You cannot appeal against the other parts of the Record — the "assessment profile" (*part 3a*), or the measures proposed (*part 5*). By appealing successfully against the other parts of the record, it may be possible to get these other parts changed, however. You can also express your disagreement with any part of the Record when stating your point of view in part 7 of the Record.

The education authority must inform you of your rights of appeal. It will do so when informing you of its decision to record. You must be given 28 days in which to lodge your appeal, starting from the day after (weekends excepted) the authority's letter was posted to you.

Since young persons or, in certain cases, their parents are entitled to have the Record discontinued, appealing against the continuation of the Record after school leaving age will not arise. It also follows that a Record of Needs cannot be *opened* for young persons against their wishes (or those of their parents, should the young person be deemed incapable of expressing their wishes). It is still possible for young people (or their parents) to appeal against a decision *not* to open or continue a Record, however.

The diagram overleaf explains the appeals process

SPECIAL EDUCATIONAL NEEDS: APPEALS

You can appeal against:

- a decision to record
- a decision not to record
- a decision to continue or discontinue a Record of Needs (after review)
- certain parts of the Record:

    Pt. 3(b). summary of impairments.

    Pt. 4: statement of special educational needs.

    Pt. 6: the school named by the education authority, provided that a placing request has already been made.

You cannot appeal again within 12 months.

Your appeal goes to:

THE APPEAL COMMITTEE

The Committee can only decide on the school to be attended. All other matters must be referred to the Secretary of State for a decision.

You must be given 28 days in which to appeal.

You can attend the Appeal in person, appeal in writing or do both. You can bring up to three other people with you.

At least one of the Appeal Committee members should be a parents' representative.

SHERIFF COURT

You have a further right of appeal to the Court against a decision by the Appeal Committee about the school to be attended. The Court must, however, refer your appeal to the Secretary of State if it thinks that a decision by him is also involved.

SECRETARY OF STATE

Secretary of State's decision is final and must be referred back to the Appeal Committee (or Sheriff Court), which must then decide on the school to be attended in the light of that decision.

Circumstances in which you might want to appeal

Example
You do not want your child to go to a special school, class or unit.

You can appeal against:
A decision to record *or* part 6 of the Record *or* both, but possibly against parts 3b or 4 of the Record as well.

You want your child to go to a special school, class or unit.

Normally a decision *not* to record *or* part 6 of the Record, if opened.

You disagree with the assessment of your child's difficulties or requirements.

Parts 3b *or* 4 of the Record *or* both.

You want your child to receive specialist or extra help with his or her education, whether in an ordinary or a special school.

A decision *not* to record

You disagree with the measures proposed to help your child.

You *cannot* appeal against this, but by appealing successfully against parts 3b, 4 and/or 6, you may be able to get part 5 changed.

Please note that the decision to record or not is different from a decision to place a child in a special school or not; a decision to record could still mean your child can go to an ordinary school, depending on the school named in part 6 of the record.

Preparing your appeal

When preparing your appeal:

- Work out with the help of a solicitor, your Named Person (if any) and anybody else concerned exactly what it is you are appealing against, as this could affect the way your appeal is handled. Is your appeal against the assessment of your child's difficulties or requirements alone, regardless of the school proposed for your child? Do you agree with the assessment of your child's difficulties or requirements but disagree with the school proposed? Your answers could affect whether you appeal against the recording decision itself, the content of the record, or both.

- Check whether you and your solicitor and Named Person have all the relevant information (letters, documents, reports) to support your case. The education authority must send to you any information considered relevant to its decision at least ten days before the hearing. It must also give you any other relevant information the appeal committee asks for before or during the hearing.

- Decide whether you want to put your appeal in writing, appear in person at the hearing or to do both. Any written submissions must be sent to the appeal committee and the education authority at least ten days before the hearing. If you decide to appear in person, do you want to be accompanied by anybody — for example, your Named Person, solicitor, or other advisor?

- Note down all you want to say at the hearing, setting out your objections, arguments or evidence in support of your point of view (this could include reference to any assessments carried out privately for you). Try to anticipate the claims or point of view of the education authority.

- Keep in mind that the appeal committee can only make a decision about whether or not to uphold your choice of school — any other matter which you or the committee raise and which touches on the assessment and recording of your child must be referred to the Secretary of State.

- In presenting your case, do not hesitate to:

  - call upon as witnesses sympathetic professional staff or voluntary workers who know your child or understand his or her difficulties.

  - refer to any assessments you have had carried out privately, submitting written reports if possible as well.

  - draw attention to any reports, such as the Warnock report, or statements of policy or actual practices of your education authority which appear to support your point of view.

  - suggest alternative approaches to your child's education, especially if this is not likely to involve the authority spending a lot more money.

At the hearing (if you decide to attend) try to remain calm, patient, tactful and hopeful. Those listening to your appeal will understand and may well share your concerns, so that little is likely to be gained by allowing your distress to interfere with the presentation of your case.

Referring appeals to the Secretary of State

Your child's case will be referred to special educational and medical advisers* appointed to recommend to the Secretary of State whether or not your child should be recorded, or whether the statements in the Record about your child's difficulties or requirements need to be altered in some way. Your own views must be taken into consideration in recommending what action the Secretary of State should take. The Secretary of State does not decide on the school to be attended — the committee dealing with your appeal is responsible for this in the light of his decision.

The Secretary of State's advisers will look at all the information and reports about your child's assessment, including any written statements or reports you make yourself. They will arrange to meet you and give you a chance to explain why you do or do not want a Record of Needs for your child or why you disagree with something in the Record. You could also ask your Named Person (if you have one) or someone else (for example, from a voluntary organisation) to come along to the meeting. You are, of course, free to give your views in writing as well.

The Secretary of State's advisers will probably want to see and talk to your child as well as listen to your own views. They will want to find out as much as possible about your child and his or her difficulties and requirements. Anything you tell them will be treated in confidence and they will want to understand your point of view in making recommendations to the Secretary of State. There is no time limit within which the Secretary of State must reach his decision.

The Secretary of State can order the education authority to:

discontinue your child's Record of Needs. The authority must then arrange for your child to attend a suitable school, taking account of your wishes.

open a Record of Needs. The authority will then have to record your child's special needs, what special help to offer and where your child should be educated, in the light of the Secretary of State's decision.

alter something in parts 3b (summary of impairments) or 4 (statements of special educational need) in the Record. This could

---

*These special advisers, who are likely to be inspectors from the Scottish Education Department and government medical advisers, should not be confused with the educational advisers appointed by education authorities.

result in the education authority having to alter parts 5 (measures proposed) and 6 (school to be attended) as well.

The Secretary of State's decision on the above matters is final. The committee dealing with your appeal must be notified of his decision. It must then decide, in the light of that decision, the school (if any) to be attended. It must allow your child to attend the school of your own choice if satisfied, in the light of the Secretary of State's decision, that the authority was not justified in turning down your placing request. You have a further right of appeal against the committee's decision to the Sheriff Court. The sheriff must take into account the decision of the Secretary of State when considering your appeal. The sheriff cannot deal with appeals against the recording decision itself; he can only deal with appeals insofar as they relate to choice of school.

What happens if your appeal is unsuccessful?

If your appeal is referred to the Secretary of State for a decision, then that decision is final.* You can, however, ask the education authority to review its recording decision (or review the content of the Record) 12 months after that decision. If you disagree with the appeal committee's decision about the school your child should attend, you can take your appeal to the sheriff court. You normally have 28 days in which to do this. Your case will be heard in private.

Should you appeal to the sheriff, the court must take any decision by the Secretary of State into account before deciding whether to grant you the school of your choice. If the court considers that a decision by the Secretary of State is required and this has not been sought, then the sheriff must refer your appeal to the Secretary of State; only after the Secretary of State has reached a decision can the court then deal with your appeal. The sheriff's decision is final.

---

* You could also consider making a formal complaint to the Secretary of State that the education authority is failing in its duty to provide adequate and efficient education (or take the authority to court yourself). Get legal advice about this. See also the sections on "Complaints" and "Legal Action" in *The Law of the School*.

How are a child's special educational needs monitored?

If your child has been recorded, then the education authority must follow certain legally laid down procedures for keeping regular watch over your child's special needs. This is necessary in order to take account of any new or changing needs your child might have or with a view to discontinuing the record if your child can now manage well enough without special help. Even if your child has not been recorded, however, you should still expect the authority or the school to be on the alert for any children likely to have special needs which may call for a recording decision later on, for example, as a result of deterioration in their physical, mental or emotional condition. In the case of recorded children, the authority must, whenever it thinks necessary, conduct a formal review of its own to find out whether it should continue keeping a Record of Needs or whether your child's needs have changed in any way so as to call for an alteration to the record. It must also conduct a formal review if you as parent ask for one; the authority must normally agree to do so unless there has already been a formal review in the previous 12 months.

The review process

The review process basically follows the same procedures as when a child is assessed and recorded for the first time:

- you must be told that your child is to be assessed

- you must be given 21 days to give your point of view

- you must be asked if you want additional assessments carried out; the authority must normally arrange to have this done.

As before, the authority must consider all reports and recommendations made by people assessing your child. It must also consider your own views about what should be done and when. Refer back to section pages 27-34 for guidance about how you can help here.

Before reaching a final decision, the education authority must tell you about:

- its decision to continue or discontinue the Record of Needs for your child and the reasons for doing so

- any proposed changes to the content of the Record of Needs

- your right to ask for a choice of school if the school named in the Record of Needs is to be changed.

The authority must give you 14 days in which to give your views, which it must consider carefully before reaching a final decision about any changes proposed. You must be told of your rights to appeal once the authority has decided whether to continue or discontinue recording your child. You appeal in the same way as with an initial decision to record. You can also appeal against any changes to parts 3b, 4 or 6 of the Record.

What about education for special needs after school leaving age?*

Assessment of future educational needs

Before your child reaches school leaving age, about age 16, the education authority must carry out what is called a "future needs assessment". This is to find out what educational and training opportunities your child would benefit from, such as a course at a college of further education. Between the time your child reaches the age of 14 and 15 years 3 months, the authority must prepare a report saying whether your child:

> would benefit from staying on at school beyond the school leaving age, as he or she is entitled to do.

> should continue to be recorded if staying on at school.

The authority will send you a copy of this report, saying what it thinks should be done, at least six months before your child reaches school leaving age. The report may only *recommend* what should be done — only the Record of Needs, if continued, says what the authority *must* provide beyond school leaving age to help a young person with his or her education.

In drawing up this report, the education authority may carry out any medical, psychological or other assessments which they or you think are necessary. It may also make use of reports or advice from school teachers, careers, or guidance staff, disablement settlement officers, training agencies, the health board, social work departments or voluntary bodies.

The education authority must give you at least 21 days to state your own views — and those of your child — about your child's future needs. Before finalising its report it must consider carefully your views and any reports you may present. It is expected to discuss the contents of the report with both you and your child. You may be asked to comment on it and a copy will be sent to you, usually six months or so before your child reaches school leaving age. Copies may also be sent to the health board, social work department or, with your permission, to

---

* For further information, see *A College Guide: meeting special educational needs in Scotland*, by Liz Sutherland, National Bureau for handicapped students, 1987.

another body, such as a voluntary organisation involved with your child. (A copy must be sent to the health and social work authorities, in the case of disabled pupils, six months before your child reaches school leaving age.) You must be told about your right to have the Record of Needs discontinued once your child has reached school leaving age.

Assessment of social and welfare needs

Under the Disabled Persons (Services, Consultation and Representation) Act 1986, disabled people have rights to be represented or consulted about matters relating to their welfare when local authorities are planning or providing services, including educational services — although the full educational implications of this act, at the time of writing, as yet remain unclear. The Act also requires education and social work authorities to keep under review the cases of all children and young people who have been assessed by them.

The education authority must notify the social work department to say whether your child is disabled or not, and, if so, put this down in the Record of Needs and in its report on your child's future educational needs.* The social work department must then assess your child, if disabled, to work out and prepare a report on what help should be provided, through its statutory services, for his or her future care and welfare. This assessment will have to be carried out either:

- when your child, is between 14 and $15^1/_4$ years old that is, at around the same time as the future needs assessment. Education and social work departments are expected to carry out their assessments jointly, so as to minimise the stress parents may be under at this time.

    or

- as soon as is reasonably practicable, but within six months of the education authority asking the social work authority whether or not your child is disabled. The assessment could take place before your child reaches school leaving age but might not be until he or she is 16 or 17. The social work authority need not carry out the assessment, however, if your child has reached 16 and he or she has requested it not to do so (or if, due to the mental or physical incapacity of the child, the parent has so requested).

---

* The Act defines a disabled person as a chronically sick, physically disabled or mentally disordered person in need of local authority social welfare services. Most children with special educational needs which have been recorded are covered by the Act. For further details see Circular SW2/1988 SED/1167, issued jointly by the Social Work Services Group and the Scottish Education Department, 13 January 1988.

The education authority must let the social work department know the date by which a disabled child or young person is no longer receiving full time school or further education.

Under the Mental Health (Scotland) Act 1984, local authorities have a duty to provide or secure suitable training or work (for example, in sheltered workshops), for the young people over school age who are not in school or further education, except if they are in hospital.

Making your views known about your child's future needs

When discussing your child's future needs with professional and other staff, you should expect to be as fully involved as possible before any decisions are reached. Your child should also be encouraged to take an active part if he or she is clearly capable of doing so. You should also expect a *comprehensive* picture of your child's future needs — educational, career, social, emotional, health, and so on — to be drawn up. Education, careers advice, social work, counselling, disablement resettlement, health and other professionals should all be involved, if necessary, depending on your child's difficulties. Your Named Person, if you have one, could also be expected to take part.

Although the law does not say what the future needs assessment should cover, you should expect consideration to be given to each of the following aspects of your child's future after 16.

- Arrangements for educating your child after 16. In school? College? Youth Training Scheme? Special training centre? Day release course? If your child has shown little promise at school, do not assume that there is no point in continuing with his or her education after 16. There is plenty of evidence to show people with difficulties can continue learning at their own pace right into adulthood.

- Arrangements for providing your child with careers guidance, help in finding a suitable job or choosing a suitable training course. Advice should come from either ordinary careers officers or special career advisers and people, such as disablement resettlement officers, familiar with your child's needs. Again, do not assume that your child should accept "second best" opportunities or "second rate" jobs simply on account of his or her disability. Your child's adjustment to a particular career or job may depend as much on how accommodating employers are as on your child's ability to adapt.

- Where appropriate, provisions for giving your child continued or further training in basic practical or "life skills", such as writing job applications, making telephone calls, handling money, finding somewhere to live and so on. School guidance, careers and other staff often provide courses on these matters before children are due to leave school and you should expect this sort of preparation to continue at school or college long after your child has reached 16, depending on how serious your child's difficulties are.

- Special provisions for children who have lost a lot of schooling, due to illness, disability and other factors, by the time they are due to leave school. This could include allowing your child to repeat a course or resit an exam, perhaps with additional tuition in order to do so.

- Continuation of support such as therapy and auxiliary help while your child continues to be educated after 16 at school or college.

If your child continues to be recorded at age 16 and 17, specialist help with his or her education will carry on being provided; even if the Record is discontinued, the school or college may still carry on providing specialist help or support. After leaving school your child, and possibly yourself as parent as well, may still need counselling and other expert help, guidance and support about decisions affecting your child's future, such as ones connected with:

- finding and settling down in a job or a course of study.

- leaving home and learning to look after oneself (where practicable).

- developing new friends, interests, pastimes and so on.

More and more emphasis is now being placed on giving people with disabilities a better chance to live in the ordinary community instead of being confined to institutions or housebound all the time. You should expect the education services to play a full part in this process, which, while not enforceable by law, should cover things like giving people with various disabilities encouragement and special opportunities to take part in further and adult education classes and cultural, sporting and recreational activities. You may be able to get services changed or improved by making your views known to those responsible for representing the interests of disabled people in the planning or running of services: for example, in education and recreation. Contact your local authority for the names and address of suitable contacts.

Part Two:
Working out what your child's special needs are

Introduction

"The child who is physically, mentally or socially handicapped shall be given the special treatment, education and care required by his particular condition". *United Nations Declaration of the Rights of the Child*, principle 5.

This part of the handbook tells you what sort of additional help or support your child may need to get the best out of his or her education. The sort of support needed will be worked out whenever your child is expertly assessed (see pages 27 to 34) but the actual help provided will also depend on:

- the *policies, practices* and *resources* (money, staff, etc) of the education authority for helping children with special needs. These will vary from one authority to another. You should ask the authority for information about its policies or practices, including provisions in ordinary schools (see pages 115-120 below). Although lack of resources is not in itself a legal ground for limiting or refusing the help your child may require, it is unlikely that the education authority will be ordered to do something beyond its power to achieve, should your case go to court.

- whether or not it is the policy of the education authority to *record* particular difficulties for the purpose of providing special help. Some of the difficulties described below will be recorded if they are considered pronounced, specific or complex as to call for specialist support, perhaps over a long period; other more moderate difficulties may go unrecorded and may or may not benefit from specialist support.

- *which school(s)* you can send your child to (see pages 35-40 and 123-28)

- the outcome of any *appeals* you might make (see pages 52-58)

- whether the education authority or school is in a position to offer extra help to children with learning difficulties or other special needs which have *not* been recorded — the great majority of children with special educational needs are in this situation.

This section starts off by describing the general range of additional or specialist help which may be given, followed by more detailed sections about support for children with particular difficulties. Each section describes the general nature of the particular difficulty and then goes on to suggest ways in which support may be provided. For more detailed advice, however, you should consult one or more of the specialist organisations or publications listed at the end of this handbook.

Sources of children's difficulties at school

Children's special needs vary greatly in cause and character, but the main sources of children's learning and other difficulties are likely to stem from one or more of the following:

- inappropriate curricula (what is taught) and teaching methods and, more generally, the failure of the education system to respond to the child's needs

- children's abilities and aptitudes

- children's motivation to learn, having regard to any social or emotional problems children may be having, including parents' attitudes and support from the home, which is known to be related to children's educational progress

- any physical or sensory impairments children have, such as difficulties in hearing, movement, speaking, seeing or perceiving, and so on

- a combination of the above factors.

Each of these factors varies considerably in severity, complexity and scope. For example, learning difficulties range from difficulties in grasping ideas or concepts or learning particular skills (affecting a large proportion of children) to basic difficulties in learning at all, at the most elementary level (affecting only a very small percentage of children). Some social or emotional difficulties may be temporary or short-lived, while others may be deep rooted and call for intensive support, perhaps throughout schooling. Some physical or sensory impairments may call for only a very limited amount of special provision, such as adaptations to school premises or equipment, while others may require specialist teaching or support. The environment in which children grow up and learn will also exert a very important influence on how children learn and cope at school, with any learning or other difficulties children have being very much relative to the support they get in the home and at school. These points should be borne in mind when reading the sections which follow.

Help and support for your child

As a parent, you have a legal responsibility to see that your child is properly educated, normally by seeing that your child attends school regularly or, in exceptional cases, by arranging for your child to be educated by other means, for example, by being educated at home. Since your own attitudes may affect your child's motivation to learn, you will also want to give your child as much support and encouragement as possible, for example, by taking an interest in his or her schoolwork, meeting school staff to discuss your child's progress, and generally co-operating with the school to promote your child's well-being.

Equally, though, you should expect a certain amount of help and support to come from the education authority in fulfilling its legal duty to secure "adequate and efficient" education and to provide education according to your child's age, ability, aptitudes and his or her special educational needs (whether recorded or not). The assessment and recording of your child, where this applies, should represent the best possible attempt to put this principle into practice. As explained above, though, whether your child will get the help he or she requires could well depend on such factors as the policies and resources of the education authority or the success of any appeals you might make. It is therefore very important that you find out all you can about what your child's requirements are, with reference to this part of the handbook and by speaking to staff and others concerned, in case what is proposed for your child should turn out to be different from what your child requires.

Checklist of suitable measures to help your child

- **Early detection, diagnosis, referral and support**. As soon as your child's difficulties become apparent, you should expect the education authority to be informed and act promptly to assess, if necessary, your child's special needs, under the procedures described in pages 27-34 above. You should arrange, if possible, to be present at any meetings related to assessments of your child to make your point of view and concerns known.

- **Pre-school education**. To ensure that your child is given the best possible start before formal schooling begins at the age of $4^1/_2$ to $5^1/_2$ years approximately, you should expect some sort of pre-school educational help to be provided. This may mean your child joining a nursery school or class or playgroup from the age of two or three, perhaps combined with home visits from a specialist teacher. Pre-school education is also important in discovering any difficulties of your child which have, so far, gone unnoticed.

- **Supportive school environment**. To enable children with special needs to settle down and feel at ease, the school should make every effort to be adaptable, flexible and supportive in its approach. Support could include specialist or extra tuition, flexible timetabling, teaching in small groups, sensitive layout or positioning of school apparatus, and so on. It should also include the promotion of appropriate attitudes among other pupils and staff and generally making the school a warm and friendly place to be in.

- **Close links between home and school**. Parents of children with special needs should be given every encouragement to visit school, meet specialist staff where appropriate and become fully involved in their child's education. Where a child's difficulties result in frequent absences from school, contact with parents may be maintained through home visits from school staff.

- **Specialist tuition**. For children whose difficulties prevent ordinary communication between teacher and pupil, specialist instruction, for example in sign language, may be appropriate. Specialist tuition may also be necessary for children with social or emotional problems. Specialist tuition need not affect what is taught (see below) — children receiving specialist tuition may still be able to follow a normal curriculum, although this may, out of necessity, have to be modified.

- **Modified curricula** (what is taught). Where children have difficulty in learning or understanding what is taught, the curriculum may be modified to fit in with a more appropriate pace of learning, more relevant work, children's motivation, interests, background, and so on.

- **Counselling**. Guidance or support may be offered to children and their families to help them cope with any social or emotional difficulties they face. Counsellors, social workers, psychologists, and so on, may visit or be attached to schools to give support. In secondary schools, specialist teachers of guidance should also be available for pupils and parents to see.

- **Suitable adaptations** to help children in such things as moving around school or in classrooms, using materials and equipment, taking part in practical activities and so on. This could include provision of such things as ramps, special seating, handrails, modified worktops and other furnishings, special handgrips on equipment, additional lighting and so on.

- **Aids or equipment** to assist with such learning tasks as reading, writing, listening, practical work, music, physical education and so on. Aids could include special typewriters, computers, listening devices, microphone links, paper holds, tools, PE equipment, etc.

- **Examinations**. Children with special needs could be given extra time in which to complete exams or practical help in presenting their answers. Special arrangements already exist for pupils with special needs to sit SCE exams, for example, provision of extra time, a scribe to write down answers, braille equipment for blind candidates, and so on.

- **Auxiliary help**. This could be given for such practical tasks as eating, dressing, toileting, moving about the school, lifting or reaching for things, operating equipment, medication, and so on.

- **Safety arrangements**. School staff are under a legal duty to take whatever reasonable measures are necessary to ensure the safety of pupils in their care. While this obligation is not absolute, special efforts should be made to care for children whose difficulties put them at greater risk of accident or injury compared with other children. Without being "overprotective", schools can do the following sorts of things to maximise safety:

  providing adaptations to equipment so as to lessen the risk of accident, such as fitting laboratory equipment with special stabilisers

  taking steps to promote the safe use of articles such as sharp instruments, safe positioning of apparatus and so on

  attaching special instructions or warning signs to articles or equipment for the benefit of children who cannot follow ordinary instructions

  developing school and classroom routines for all pupils, such as movement about corridors or in class to reduce the risk of accidental injury

  personal help from teaching or auxiliary staff with lifting or reaching for things, operating equipment, using apparatus, or movement about school buildings

  emergency procedures for evacuating children with particular difficulties in the event of fire supervision of children with particular difficulties in playgrounds or on school trips

most important of all, raising the level of consciousness among staff and fellow pupils about the safety of children with particular difficulties.

- **Arrangements** for children with particular difficulties to:

  take part in school trips, extra-curricula, sporting and social activities

  visit doctors, dentists, clinics, etc. during school hours

  attend special courses, work experience schemes and other educational activities outside school.

- **Help after school leaving age**. If your child stays on at school beyond school leaving age (age 16 approx.), additional help should continue to be provided, and must do so for as long as a young person at school continues to be recorded. Even if your child's special needs have not been recorded or if the record has been discontinued (for example as a result of your child leaving school to start college), additional help may still be available. It is worth checking with your education authority first, or with the school(s) or college(s) concerned, to see what help can be given. For more detailed information, refer to *A College Guide: meeting special educational needs in Scotland* and other publications listed at the end of this handbook.

Learning difficulties

Children and young people who have significantly greater difficulties
in learning compared with the majority of others of their own age
represent the largest proportion of pupils with special educational
needs. Learning difficulties vary enormously in cause and character,
from difficulties in acquiring the most elementary intellectual, physical
or social skills, affecting only a very small percentage of children, to

specific problems with particular tasks like number and reading work, affecting a considerably large proportion of children. Some of the more pronounced difficulties are inherited at birth, as with Down's syndrome, or may be due to brain injury before, during, or after birth. Others may have no obvious physical causes but may arise from lack of proper stimulation, arising from, say, lack of social support or inappropriate learning opportunities. In some cases, children with learning difficulties may have physical disabilities or emotional problems which may affect their learning as well.

Understanding children's learning difficulties

Traditionally many children with learning difficulties have been labelled as "backward", "dull", "defective", "retarded", "slow", "sub-normal" and so on, depending on the severity of their difficulty. In recent years there has been a movement away from putting children into watertight categories like this, on the grounds that:

- there are no clear dividing lines between children of so-called normal intelligence and those of below average intelligence who have only mild or moderate learning difficulties. There is even disagreement about what "intelligence" is — with some experts saying it is whatever intelligence tests measure!

- many learning difficulties may not originate with the child at all, but may arise from poor or unsuitable schooling, inappropriate curricula or teaching methods, difficult home circumstances, cultural differences, language difficulties and so on.

- no child is ineducable; even children with the severest difficulties, given the right kind of stimulus and encouragement, can make progress in ways relevant and appropriate to their own needs and abilities.

- labelling a child in this way could be educationally and socially harmful as well as distressing to parents; it wrongly places emphasis on what a child cannot do properly to the exclusion of what he or she can do well. Children with learning difficulties can still make good progress in reading and written work, given the right kind of teaching and support.

- learning difficulties are relative to the knowledge and skills society demands of people; people living in a society where literacy, numeracy and other complex skills are deemed important are more likely to be regarded as having learning difficulties than in societies where they are less important.

A report[*] by the Inspectorate some years ago in fact indicated that the term learning difficulty could be applied to a much wider and more diverse range of pupils than had been supposed:

> "It extends well beyond those pupils who have difficulty in learning anything at all to include those who have difficulty in coping with ideas and concepts, not to mention the language in which those ideas and concepts are expressed. It also applies to those pupils whose problems are the result of, for example, frequent absence or change of school." (para 4.2)

Learning difficulties thus may relate to any one or more of the following:

- functioning physically, learning through practice or experience, responding to one's surroundings

- understanding meanings of words, or symbols, memorising, grasping ideas, reasoning, making connections, problem solving, and so on

- recognising shapes, sizes, pictures or configurations, sound patterns, etc; relating objects to one another, judging distances and so on

- communicating with others, developing orderly behaviour, carrying out routine everyday tasks.

Not all of these difficulties need be due to limited ability; some may arise from emotional disturbance, physical disability (such as difficulties in hearing or seeing), or inappropriate instruction. These difficulties may vary from mild to severe; some may be overcome with the right sort of special help, while others may be lifelong and require continuing support; most probably lie somewhere between these extremes.

Many of these difficulties are likely to affect how children learn to build up vocabulary, read and write, handle and measure quantities and shapes, draw comparisons and connections, conduct experiments, and more generally do things and find out things for themselves. However, children with even the severest difficulties may be able to progress in such things as talking, recognising key words, numbers, signs or symbols, or doing straightforward practical tasks.

---

[*] Scottish Education Department, *The Education of Pupils with Learning Difficulties in Primary and Secondary Schools in Scotland*, HMSO 1980.

Special help may comprise:

- pre-school education at home, in nursery schools, playgroups or in special classes or units well before the child starts compulsory education at age 5 approximately.

- modified curriculum tailored to the child's particular learning difficulties, such as work in reading, arithmetic, vocabulary, observation, etc.

- specialist tuition, whether in ordinary or special classes, geared to the child's own pace of learning, attention span, and so on.

- creation of school surroundings which are comfortable and stimulating for the child to learn in, such as making schools and classrooms easy to find one's way around in and places with lots of things to do.

- training in everyday skills and tasks, work experience for older pupils, cultivation of special pursuits, timetabling of school activities in a varied and flexible way.

- lots of patience, empathy and support from school staff, with a readiness to vary their teaching methods according to the very individual needs of each child.

- plenty of opportunity and encouragement for parents, to visit the school, watch their child at work, and be regularly informed of progress.

All these things are the hallmarks of any good school and should not be reserved only for children with learning difficulties. There is, nonetheless, a need for schools to pay special attention to these practices when faced with any children who have much greater difficulty in learning than their fellows.

Most children with 'mild' learning difficulties will probably benefit from an ordinary curriculum (what is taught) and be able to participate in ordinary classroom activities, but they will need more individual attention and may have to join special classes or units attached to an ordinary school some of the time, for example, for reading and number work.

These special classes or units may form part of the ordinary school buildings, but they may also be housed in separate buildings or wings of the school. Children with profound or severe learning difficulties may need to attend a special school, but it may be possible for them to join special classes or units at an ordinary school instead. The type of support offered or available will vary from school to school and also depend on the policies of the education authority, but every effort should be made for pupils with learning difficulties to mix with other children from ordinary classes as much as possible.

Emotional and social difficulties

Children with various emotional and social difficulties may also have special educational needs that call for a lot of expert help and support. Their difficulties may arise from a whole range of circumstances, such as an unsettled home background, relationships with other people, illness, and so on. Some difficulties may be temporary, others long lasting. Many children are believed to go through emotional and social difficulties at some time during their schooling. Their difficulties could affect:

- their ability to concentrate in class.

- their attendance at school/participation in school activities.

- their willingness to fit in with school discipline.

These difficulties could result in serious "underachievement". They may call for one or more of the following sorts of special help for a limited or extended period of time, with a view to a gradual return to ordinary class where applicable.

- Special attention from the psychology service of the education authority; individual tuition and observation in special classes or units attached to an ordinary school; or, in some cases, attendance at a special residential school for disturbed children. Such children may be taught in very small groups, of perhaps less than 6 to 10 pupils.

- Modified curricula, special classrooms and timetabling of lessons carefully tailored to the needs and interests of the child.

- Tolerance, patience and insight on the part of school staff, supportive emotional climate at school.

- Close links with the home or whoever is in charge of the child outside school hours.

- Close contact with social workers, psychologists, educational welfare officers, and others concerned with the child; specialist counselling with pupils or their families, including support in crisis situations.

"Punishing" or "excluding" children from school should be seen as an inappropriate or short-term solution to the emotional or social difficulties children are having.

Hearing difficulties

Hearing loss or difficulty may stem from various causes, physical and non-physical, and extend to problems in listening, limited attention spans, language difficulties — or even be due to the teacher not speaking clearly or loud enough!

- not being able to hear at all, with associated speech or language difficulties if the hearing loss occurred at birth or soon after. Children who become deaf later on may have fewer speech or language difficulties.

- children with partial hearing, who cannot hear sounds properly in terms of their loudness, pitch or range. Some children may have difficulties in hearing or distinguishing between certain word or letter sounds.

- children who can hear properly but have difficulty in listening to or concentrating on what is said, because of language barriers, poor concentration, emotional disturbance or other factors.

These difficulties may affect children's speech, pronunciation, or use of spoken language and may have associated effects on their learning or on social and personality development. Children vary considerably, however, in their ability to cope with deafness or hearing difficulties, depending on their natural abilities, personality and other factors, so that the amount of hearing loss should not be assumed to have a proportionate effect on their educational progress. There are special schools for deaf children, but it is possible for children with hearing difficulties to be educated in ordinary schools as well, given special help and support there.

Specialist help

Help could include one or more of the following:

- Early screening for hearing difficulties as soon as possible after birth (8-10 months) and regularly thereafter, both before and after starting school.

- Provision of suitable hearing aids, possibly linked up with a radio microphone system in class.

- Lip-reading or sign language in lesson, including the use of "interpreters" in ordinary class.

- Auditory training, helping children to recognise sounds, possibly combined with speech practice.

- Language tuition, tuition in slow or special English.

- Written lesson notes and instructions.

- Visits from specialist teachers of deaf or partially hearing children.

- Suitable positioning of children and teacher in class.

- Good acoustic conditions inside school, such as properly soundproofed classrooms.

- Warning lights and other signs to show that machinery, schoolbells, fire alarm, etc., are in operation.

- Counselling and support for example, to promote self-confidence.

- Group activities to reduce social isolation and the 'stigma' commonly associated with hearing difficulties.

- Appropriate attitudes by other pupils and staff, who may be inclined to be less tolerant about 'deafness', compared with other difficulties.

Medical disorders

Children with certain illnesses or medical disorders may be in need of as much help as children with physical disabilities or learning difficulties. Any of the following conditions may call for some sort of additional support with schooling:

Anemia
Arthritis
Breathing difficulties
Brittle Bones
Cerebral Palsy*
Coeliac condition
Cystic fibrosis*
Diabetes
Epilepsy*
Friedreich's ataxia*
Haemophilia

Heart or kidney disorders
Incontinence
Leukaemia
ME post-viral syndrome*
Mental Illness
Muscular dystrophy*
Migraine
Nerve disorders
Severe allergic conditions
Serious head injury
Skin diseases
Spina bifida*
Spinal injuries

Some of the above conditions may result in frequent or prolonged absence from school, depending on the sort of medical attention required, although education should continue as far as possible while children are undergoing treatment in hospital or convalescing at home. More specific problems arising could include:

- Difficulties in concentrating or completing work, although these difficulties may be minimised where appropriate medication or practical assistance is given.

- Limited participation in things like school sport, school trips, or other activities in which pupils may use up a lot of energy, although this should *not* normally be necessary for children with conditions like diabetes if appropriate medication, food supplements, etc., can be given.

- Difficulties in body control, holding things, handling equipment, moving about, writing etc.

* See pages 95-99 for further information

Specialist help

Special help could include one or more of the following:

- Special arrangements for medication to be given, or for school doctors, nurses or auxiliary staff to be in attendance at appropriate times.

- Modifying or relaxing the demands normally made on pupils, for example, by giving a child with a medical problem more time in which to complete work, making special allowances or exemptions in practical activities like games and PE, and so on.

- Home or hospital schooling, given by visiting or resident teachers (education authorities employ their own specialist staff for this; every effort should be made to make sure that children's education at home or in hospital adequately makes up for the loss of ordinary schooling).

- Without being overprotective, safeguarding pupils from things like sharp objects, irritants, toxic substances, extremes of temperature, air

impurities, building defects, etc. Some pupils with conditions like asthma and migraine have alergic reactions to school pets, which may have to be kept well away from them. Children with epilepsy may be sensitive to flashing lights, especially defective fluorescent lighting.

- Provision of special or healthy diets, for example, fresh fruit instead of stodgy puddings; extra snacks for diabetic children.

- Wearing of protective clothing, for example as a safeguard against skin allergies, cuts or bruises, etc.

- Special arrangements and routines to allow safe arrival at and dismissal from school, or movement around school.

- Special arrangements or allowances for pupils with medical problems to sit examinations, for example arranging for an examination to be taken under supervision at home or in hospital.

- Fostering appropriate attitudes among staff and other pupils and their parents and perhaps making special efforts to ensure that children with medical difficulties do not retreat into isolation but are befriended, not excluded.

Mobility difficulties

Children with limited or restricted mobility represent a significant proportion of those requiring special help with their education. Their difficulties cover an enormous range.

- Complete paralysis of body.

- Limited or no use of certain parts of the body, such as hands, arms, feet or legs.

- Loss of sensation in various parts of the body which may therefore be prone to pressure sores, burns, etc., if left unprotected.

- Problems of physical co-ordination in walking, handling objects, operating equipment, etc.

- Weak or limited use of certain muscles affecting the use of hands, legs, etc., as with muscular dystrophy.

- Brittle bones or skeletal deformities/dislocations (e.g. of the spine or the hips) inhibiting movement.

Some children may have had these conditions since birth and will have had some time to adapt, but others may have become physically disabled as a result of some accident or illness later on in life and find the process of adjustment emotionally painful. Some of these disabilities may be complicated by hearing, visual speech or learning difficulties, as with many cerebral palsy or spina bifida children (see pages 95-99).

Children with these difficulties are likely to have problems in:

- getting physical access to all or parts of the school.

- taking part in certain practical activities, such as games or physical education.

- writing, handicraft, and construction work, etc.

- adapting to the physical environment — using ordinary chairs, desks and worktops, moving about the school, etc.

- concentrating long enough on certain activities without getting tired or frustrated.

Specialist help

Help offered could comprise:

- special tuition (at home or in hospital) for children who cannot attend school at all.

- special aids for reading, writing, operating equipment etc.

- physio- and occupational therapy.

- mobility aids such as artificial limbs, wheelchairs, callipers, etc.

- adaptations to school equipment and furnishings, seating, toilet and washing facilities, entrances; provision of lifts, ramps, handrails/ holds; modifications to desks and worktops, computer keyboards, instruments, etc.

- specialist counselling and social support for children and facilities to help them to come to terms with their disablement, promote self-reliance, confidence in dealing with others, planning their future, etc.

Speech or language difficulties

A significant proportion of children are believed to have difficulties in speaking or talking, which to a varying degree could affect their educational progress. While some difficulties may have a physiological cause, many may stem from social, emotional or cultural factors, including the appropriateness of the language in which children are taught at school. Difficulties cover:

- complete inability to speak, perhaps as a result of some serious injury or nervous disorder.

- difficulties in making ordinary word sounds, resulting, for example in "slurred" speech, poor pronunciation, associated with conditions like cerebral palsy and cleft palate.

- difficulties in putting words together, perhaps because of some learning difficulty, or emotional or other problem.

- difficulties affecting the child's understanding or expression of language — for example, arising from the child's cultural or social background.

- hesitant or confused speech, stuttering or stammering perhaps arising from nervousness or some emotional problem.

These difficulties may affect a child's social or emotional development, which could in turn affect learning — although it should not be assumed that speech or language difficulties necessarily affect ability to learn. It should be noted, though, that the law does not regard a child as having a learning difficulty solely because the language in which he or she is taught is different from the language or form of language at any time spoken at home.

Specialist help

Specialist help may include:

- Speech therapy and specialised learning activities that aid speech development and encourage children to express themselves. Music therapy may also be effective.

- Language tuition, instruction in a slower pace of speech, mother tongue teaching (children may be withdrawn to special classes or language units for this).

- Careful listening to children by staff for any signs of difficulty which might have gone unnoticed, especially for difficulties in understanding which are masked by ordinary speech.

- Fostering of relaxed and patient attitudes by staff and others towards children who have speech or language difficulties.

Support and encouragement from the home, spending time talking and listening to one's child, may be just as important, however, as having expert help.

Visual difficulties

Children's visual difficulties range from complete or partial loss of sight to specific problems such as difficulty in focusing, eye-hand co-ordination, and perception (ways of seeing). Some of these difficulties may have been inherited at birth, while others may have been caused by injury or illness later on. Particular difficulties include:

- Complete loss of sight (and in some children, hearing loss as well — see also under *multiple* difficulties).

- Very poor eyesight, blurred or distorted vision, inability to read print at all, though possibly with an ability to distinguish between shapes or colours.

- Problems in focusing due to long or short sight; double vision; limited range of vision; colour blindness; night blindness.

- Poor eye-hand co-ordination, resulting in such difficulties in copying down things or operating equipment.

- Difficulties in recognising (and often copying) patterns, shapes, letters or words, associated with conditions like dyslexia ("difficulty with words or symbols").

These difficulties affect children's schooling in such matters as:

- learning to read and write.

- taking part in practical lessons, such as art, cookery, craftwork, PE and games, scientific experiments, etc.

- performing everyday tasks such as moving about the school, using equipment/materials, and generally coping with ordinary surroundings.

Specialist help

Although most children with visual difficulties have normal intelligence, progress with their education could be slowed down considerably unless special help is given from an early age. Help should comprise one or more of the following:

- Early detection and diagnosis of visual difficulties on a routine basis before or shortly after children start school — even children who are 'bright' may on closer examination have eyesight difficulties affecting their education.

- Specialist tuition or modified curricula to allow children who cannot see properly to take part in the full range of ordinary educational activities.

- Use of special reading books and materials, for example ones written in braille or special print.

- Tape recorded lesson notes, "talking books".

- Special visual aids such as hand-held or standing magnifiers.

- Special or supplementary lighting, suitable positioning of desks (e.g. to minimise glare or shadow), special furniture (e.g. sloping desk tops).

- Adaptations to equipment and modifications of surroundings for safety, ease of use/movement etc.; use of closed-circuit TV (to monitor movement about the school).

- Mobility instruction (in finding one's way about).

- Proper consideration by staff and other pupils, for example in movement about the school or classroom, in face-to-face communication.

Multiple difficulties

Children with more than one major difficulty — such as autistic, blind-deaf, cerebral palsy or spina bifida children — present very specialist demands on education services. With advances in medicine, the number of such children who survive into adulthood is increasing. In some cases, arrangements may be made for children to attend a school specialising in their range of difficulties, such as schools for children with cerebral palsy. In other cases, it may be possible for children to attend ordinary school but to receive specialist educational or medical attention there. In the most difficult cases, hospital schooling may be necessary. For more detailed information parents should approach the psychological service of their education authority or one of the voluntary organisations listed at the end of this handbook.

- *Autism* Although its causes are not fully understood, autism in children is thought to be due to difficulties by the brain in interpreting stimuli, resulting in difficulties of the child in coping with his or her surroundings, with associated speech and learning difficulties. There is a special school in Scotland for autistic children, who as a rule do not respond well to ordinary schooling. Special help will normally include speech therapy, clinical observation, modified curricula and a school environment which is stable and unthreatening and which children can comprehend.

- *Cerebral palsy*. This is a disorder of the nervous system associated with varying difficulties of movement and frequently associated with other difficulties, in hearing and talking and often mental development (although about a quarter of such chidren have normal or above average mental ability). As no two children with cerebral palsy are affected in exactly the same way, the special help they require varies from individual to individual. Some attend special schools run by education authorities or by the Scottish Council for Spastics, others attend ordinary schools and classes, depending on how serious their difficulties are. Help frequently takes the form of physio- and speech therapy, including hydro-therapy (swimming exercises), and special adaptations and equipment to help with mobility or classwork. There is also growing interest in "conductive education", long established in Hungary but not currently available in Britain, which uses movement and music exercises combined with an ordinary curriculum to reduce or overcome certain difficulties (in walking, talking and writing). This treatment has also been applied to children with spina bifida. Cerebral palsy children with learning difficulties will receive special tuition as well. Auxiliary help may be needed with such matters as dressing, toileting, eating, operating equipment and so on.

- *Cystic fibrosis.* This is an inherited disorder of the lungs and digestive system, causing breathing difficulties, coughing, lung infections, malnourishment, and stunted growth. It is the most commonly inherited disorder among children in Great Britain, and many affected children do not survive into adulthood (although the chances of survival are improving). Although children with cystic fibrosis do not normally have difficulties in learning, they may have to spend a lot of time away from school, at home or in hospital. They also need special diets and supplements, medication, frequent toileting, physiotherapy and breathing exercise while at school, combined with sensitive handling by school staff. Their condition may also limit participation in physical activities or exertion in hot weather (where they are prone to exhaustion due to excessive loss of salt while perspiring). These children may experience emotional problems in connection with their condition, calling for additional help and support at school. Prolonged coughing may cause disturbance in class, although other pupils should be educated into forming tolerant attitudes about this.

- *Deaf-blindness.* Children who are both deaf and blind suffer some of the worst difficulties affecting learning and personal development. Most children in this condition are deaf and blind at birth, mainly as a result of the mother catching German measles (Rubella) in the first three months of pregnancy. Such children often have partial sight and/or hearing at birth, which can be prolonged with treatment, although there may be some deterioration later on. Rubella children may have heart and brain damage as well and/or suffer from other problems, for example, hyperactivity. Most special help with their education is concerned with developing their senses of touch, taste and smell. Sign language similar to that for deaf children is used *on* the hands of deaf-blind children. Children are also taught to communicate through special movements or gestures. Although learning may be slow, deaf-blind children can and do make progress. The only special school in Scotland for blind-deaf children is at Carmunnock, run by Strathclyde Education Authority.

- *Epilepsy.* Epilepsy is a neurological disorder, affecting about one in 200 people from infancy upwards and frequently associated with "fits" or "seizures" at irregular intervals. Epilepsy affects different people in different ways, however, but in many cases fits can be completely controlled with appropriate drug treatment. Most children with epilepsy can lead completely normal lives and follow normal schooling, but children with more severe forms of epilepsy may have more frequent major fits or seizures which are difficult to control and which may impair learning or lead to poor school attendance. Although the majority of children with epilepsy are of average intelligence, a high incidence of epilepsy is also found among children with severe learning difficulties. Some types of epilepsy also affect verbal or practical skills. Epilepsy in some cases may be related to behaviour problems. In the main, epilepsy in school can be coped with through sensitive classroom management; most fits are brief and do not require emergency medical treatment. But specialist support and appropriate surroundings may be necessary for children more severely affected.

- *Friedreich's ataxia.* This is a disorder of the nervous system which causes a weakening of the leg, arm, hand, eye and ear muscles (but not affecting brain functioning in any way). Although children in this condition do not have learning difficulties as such, frequent absences from school, mobility, speech, hearing and visual difficulties may severely limit progress and participation in ordinary class work. To make up for these difficulties, children will need specialist equipment, mobility aids, auxiliary help, physio and speech therapy, specialist counselling and possibly additional or specialist tuition (including home or hospital tutoring).

- *Head injuries.* Depending on the severity of the injury, head injuries can give rise to a multitude of problems and, in serious cases, where there is brain damage, the functioning of certain parts of the body, or speech, hearing or intelligence could be affected. The most common problem is loss of memory or poor memory, particularly short-term memory, but other difficulties could include personality change and conditions such as epilepsy. Teaching may have to be modified to include special skills training, for example, in memory, concentration or in coping with everyday demands. Close supervision or specialist counselling may also be necessary when there are serious behaviour or emotional problems.

- *Multiple injuries* (to hand, arm, legs, etc.), resulting from accidents or injuries at birth or during childhood for example, car accidents. Children with multiple injuries may have to spend long periods away from school in hospital or at home and may require regular nursing or medical attention at school. Depending on the nature and extent of their injuries, children may have difficulties in mobility, speech, hearing, seeing, learning and so on. Specialist help may be short-to-long-term, according to how well children recover. This could range from therapy, adaptations to school buildings, mobility aids, specialist equipment, auxiliary help, and so on, to attendance at special, residential or hospital schools. As these children may have difficulties in adjusting from the "ordinary" life they were once used to, a lot of specialised counselling and social support may be needed for them and their families.

- *ME (Post Viral Syndrome)*. ME (Myalgic encephalomyelitis) is a viral infection associated with fatigue, anxiety, depression, gastric upset, loss of concentration or memory, disturbed sleep, and so on, and is believed to affect over 100,000 children and adults in the UK to a varying degree. Although there is no widely effective treatment currently available, the effects of the illness can be minimised by sufferers taking plenty of rest and limited exercise, and many people do in fact make a spontaneous recovery, often within a couple of years. At its most severe, however, the illness may result in significant loss of schooling or motivation to learn. Support may include provision of suitable guidance to teaching staff about the handling of ME sufferers, specialist counselling, modified curricula, exemption from certain activities, and, perhaps in severe cases, home tuition.

- *Spina bifida and hydrocephalus*. When the bones of the spine are not closed properly, the nerves are exposed, and depending how well these nerves are protected, children may experience anything from loss of sensation in parts of the body below the spine to complete paralysis. Brain damage may also occur. Although this condition can be operated on soon after birth, children will need physiotherapy thereafter. Spina bifida commonly occurs with a build up of fluid around the brain (hydrocephalus), which could impair intelligence; a valve is frequently required to drain away the fluid. Children with these conditions may also suffer from incontinence, epilepsy, poor eye-hand co-ordination, perceptual difficulties, and concentration problems. Depending on the severity of their condition, children may need several sorts of specialist help, including auxiliary medical help, mobility or learning aids and adaptations, special tuition (if learning difficulties exist), and special counselling and support. "Conductive education" has also been used among children with spina bifida (see under *cerebral palsy* above).

Other multiple difficulties

In addition, special provision may be needed for children with multiple disabilities or impairments not covered by any of the above-mentioned conditions:

- physical disabilities or impairments combined with general or specific learning difficulties, for example, partial sight or hearing combined with intellectual impairment.

- physical disabilities or learning difficulties combined with medical, social or emotional problems, for example, mobility difficulties combined with chronic illness.

As for all other children with less complex special needs, the help provided should relate to the needs of the *whole* child, physical, intellectual, social and emotional, and not just to the condition which demands most attention. In some cases, special schooling may be necessary, but should not necessarily mean following a different curriculum (what is taught) from children at ordinary schools. In other cases, children may have to be educated at home or in hospital by home, hospital or visiting tutors.

Part Three:
Issues

Introduction

So far the handbook has explained how parents can put the law and the policies or practices of their education authority to the best possible use in connection with children's special educational needs (Part 1). It then went on to describe the sorts of specialist help which might be needed for particular difficulties (Part 2). This part of the handbook draws attention to a number of issues which parents groups, parents' representatives, school board members and others with an interest in provision for special education needs might want to discuss among themselves with a view to making their concerns known to central or local government and perhaps influencing policies.

Among issues covered are: How well is the law working? Are parents sufficiently involved or informed? Should parents send their child to an ordinary or special school? How might the role of the Named Person be improved? What further support should be given for parents of children under 5?

This handbook is less interested in providing conclusive answers to these questions than in raising the awareness of parents' groups and parents' representatives of the types of issues and problems affecting provision — issues which they might want to take up with government ministers, members of parliament, local councillors, and so on.

How satisfactory is the idea of "special educational need"?

The Warnock committee introduced the idea of "Special educational need" to focus attention on what should be done for the whole child or young person and no longer on the category of "handicap" he or she was assessed as belonging to. The committee corrected the mistaken view that children or young people could be divided into those requiring special education and those requiring ordinary education according to whether they were "handicapped" or not. Warnock believed that there were many "handicapped" children who were quite capable of coping with ordinary schooling, given the right sort of specialist help and support, rather than having to attend a special school. Although this represented something of an advance on previous thinking about the education of "handicapped" children, the idea of "special educational needs" has nonetheless presented certain difficulties.

- *It is by no means self evident what count as special educational needs.*

  At what point is a child deemed to have a difficulty in learning that is "significantly greater" than the majority of other children? Should a learning difficulty arising from cultural, linguistic or social background count as a special educational need? (As if in anticipation of this question, the law excludes from its definition of learning difficulty children who are taught in a language different from the language or form of language they speak at home).

  At what point do significant learning difficulties become complex, profound or specific enough to require recording? For example, a lot of children may have mild learning difficulties, emotional problems or medical difficulties giving rise to special needs about which there may be disagreement to record or not.

- *Whether or not children or young people have special educational needs may be a reflection of what provisions already exist for helping them and not simply a reflection of their condition.* An educational need only becomes a special need if it makes more than ordinary demands on educational services (staffing, equipment, what is taught, and so on). If it became ordinary practice for schools to be specially built, adapted or staffed for children or young people with certain difficulties, than, arguably, such pupils would no longer have special educational needs. Or, put differently, if schooling were to cater for only the ablest ten per cent of the population, then the remaining 90 per cent would have special needs.

- *When assessing whether children have special educational needs or not and whether these should be recorded, the experts may feel under some pressure to recommend help which fits in with such considerations as the efficient use of available resources (money and staff) and not simply the sort of help children actually require.* For example, it may be that a child with certain difficulties could be educated at an ordinary school, but only at considerable cost, such as having to employ an extra teacher there. If the specialist help is already available at a special school catering for those difficulties, the authority could argue that attendance of the child at that school is a more efficient use of resources. Experts may

be reluctant to make recommendations which the authority is unlikely to implement — and which may give rise to false expectations among parents — even though such practices may be officially frowned upon. They may also be reluctant to recommend approaches, which though educationally desirable in themselves, may place too great a strain on children or their families.

Although school and other professional staff will be only too well aware of these difficulties, you should expect them to be as open and honest with you in this respect when discussing with you, or with parents' groups, the special needs of pupils. This will help avoid possible misunderstanding or distrust later on. You may find that even if you are dissatisfied with the help on offer, staff will take a sympathetic view of your concerns and perhaps will support you if you want to raise the matter at a higher level, for example, with education officials or elected representatives.

Is the law working properly?

By abolishing the old categories of "handicap" and replacing "special education" with the concept "special educational need", the Education (Scotland) Act 1980, as amended by the 1981 Act, has helped to usher in a lot of the new thinking that has developed in this area over the years. It has also provided parents with important new rights to be consulted about their child's special needs and to appeal against certain decisions. Evidence given to a parliamentary committee* on the working of similar legislation for England and Wales (Education Act 1981) indicated that local education authorities there were now giving special educational needs much more attention than previously. It was far from clear, however, whether this change was due to the law itself or to the Warnock report and the climate of opinion it was associated with. The study being carried out for the Scottish Education Department by Edinburgh University education department should show, when results are published in due course, to what extent the Scottish changes in the law have borne fruit.**

Main criticisms

Criticisms of the legislation have included the law:

- *not being prescriptive enough.* Although the legal definition of special educational need is a broad and wide ranging one, it is also open to wide interpretation. Education authorities are left to work out what sorts of learning or other difficulties constitute special educational needs and which of them fall into the legal categories of "pronounced" "complex" or "specific" as to require recording. The above mentioned Edinburgh University study showed considerable variation between education authorities in the proportion of recorded to unrecorded pupils. An argument against making the laws too prescriptive is that such provision could lead to the "categorisation" of pupils again, contrary to the spirit of the Warnock report. The law also gives parents, through their appeal rights, opportunities to take issue with an authority's interpretation or implementation of the law.

---

* *Special Educational Needs: implementation of the Education Act 1981*, Third Report from the House of Commons Education, Science and Arts Committee, volume one, HMSO, 1987, (see also the summary of this, available from the Centre for Studies in Integration in Education).
** Interim findings are reported in *The Practice of Recording*, interim report 1, 1987 available from the department of education, University of Edinburgh.

- *not committing education authorities to policies for integrating "recorded" children with special needs into mainstream schooling.* The legislation for England and Wales says that pupils with a "statement" of special educational needs should as far as possible be educated alongside children in ordinary schools. No such principle is found in Scottish legislation, which places emphasis on parental choice of school to bring about a measure of integration (see pages 123 to 128 below for further discussion). As a result, not all education authorities in Scotland are committed to policies for integration. The interim report on the working of the Scottish legislation mentioned above showed that the large majority of recorded pupils (81 per cent) were still being placed in special schools, with most of them being placed there before the recording process had been completed, giving "credence to the belief that a prior decision or placement can influence the recording decision."

- *not laying down any time limits within which assessment and recording must be completed.* The length of time from the initial notification to parents to final recording may last several months: the Edinburgh University study showed that for 1986, recording time took over 4 months in nearly two thirds of cases, with 15 per cent taking 12 months or more to complete. The requirement on education authorities to record pupils "ascertained" under the previous legislation may have contributed to this.

- *not giving parents and young persons strong enough appeal rights.*
  Appeals can be made against only certain parts of the Record of
  Needs — the part saying what the child's or young person's
  difficulties and requirements are (parts 3b and 4) and which school
  (if any) should be attended (part 6). There is no right of appeal
  against the actual help the authority proposes to provide (part 5).

- *containing procedures which are confusing.* There are different time
  limits — 14, 21 or 28 days — within which parents or young people
  are allowed to make their views known or to lodge an appeal in the
  assessment, recording and review processes.

- *being too complicated for most parents and young people to understand
  properly.* The law on special educational needs in Scotland is found in
  two education Acts plus the Disabled Persons Act (Services,
  Consultation and Representation) Act 1986 and several regulations,
  leaving most professionals, and not just parents, rather bewildered.
  Although the Scottish Education Department and some education
  authorities produce publications which help parents and young
  people to understand their legal position, this may not always reach
  them in time or be detailed or comprehensive enought to cover their
  particular concerns.

The parliamentary select committee mentioned above said that the
main obstacle to putting the law into proper practice in England and
Wales had been the "lack of specific resources". A related criticism has
been that the recording of special educational needs on a case-by-case
basis had given rise to a piecemeal approach to provision in place of
long-term planning.

Changing the law

If you or a like-minded group of parents are dissatisfied with the way
the law is working, there are a number of things that could be done to
help bring about change:

- *making your views and concerns known to elected representatives and
  political parties at national level, particularly before election times and
  during the passage of legislation in parliament.* They may be persuaded
  to alter or modify their party's policies and commit themselves to
  changes in the law if elected or re-elected.

- *initiating court cases to draw attention to, or clarify, parts of the law which
  do not appear to be working properly or fairly.* This could include taking a
  case to the Court of Session or the European Court of Human Rights
  if it was felt that a particular practice was denying a child or young
  person with special needs a right to an adequate education. The

sections on "Complaints" and "Legal Action" in the SCC's *The Law of the School* (HMSO Books, 1987) explain this in more detail.

- *getting a member of parliament to present a "private member's" bill to change the law.* While most private members' bills are unsuccessful, they do at least ensure that the changes sought after get some public and parliamentary attention; they may encourage the government of the day to take an issue seriously. One successful example of a private member's bill becoming law is the Disabled Persons (Services, Consultation and Representation) Act 1986, which among other things gives disabled people rights to representation and consultation in the provision of social work and other welfare services.

How should parents be involved?

The Warnock report saw parents and professionals working in equal "partnership" for the successful education of children with special needs.

> "Parents can be effective partners only if professionals take notice of what they say and how they express their needs, and treat their contributions as intrinsically important. Even where parents are unable to contribute a great deal themselves, at any rate to start with, their child's welfare will depend upon the extent to which they understand and can apply the measures recommended by professionals and can help to monitor their effects. Parents will often be able to point to an aspect that the professional has overlooked or insufficiently considered." (para 9.6)

The report went on to state:

> "No assessment of a child's needs can be complete without the information which his parents can supply and no educational programme prescribed to meet his needs can be complete without their co-operation ... As a general rule parents should be included in the assessment procedures from the earliest stages and informed of the results ..." (para 4.99)

In its official guidance to education authorities, the Scottish Education Department expects parents to be treated as "equal partners" by those assessing their children, by making their thinking and conclusions known and clear to parents. Evidence given to the parliamentary select committee mentioned above indicated that so far as England and Wales was concerned parental involvement in this process had so far been rather limited. The most common complaint was that parents were not given enough information or opportunity to contribute to the assessment process, or being told enough about how their child could be helped. The Edinburgh University study should indicate, when completed in due course, how far this is the case in Scotland.

Questions parents might wish to raise among themselves at this stage include:

- are professional staff as open and communicative as they might be? Are they approachable enough?

- are parents given enough encouragement to talk over their child's difficulties and needs with school and specialist staff?

- are parents allowed to see and discuss specialists' reports on their child?

- are parents given enough guidance about taking part in the assessment and recording process?

Are parents and young people given enough written information?

Written information is very important for parents and young people if they are to take an informed part in decisions affecting their child's or their own educational future and generally understand what their school is trying to do. Parents and young people now have various sources of written information* they can turn to, much of it written with them in mind and some of it about education for special needs:

School information for parents

All publicly-run schools and independent schools offering assisted places, including special schools, must provide a range of information, which is usually put into a school handbook, saying what their arrangements for educating pupils are. This must include information about what is taught, how children's progress is assessed and reported to parents and what arrangements there are for parents to visit school. Special schools must also say in their handbooks what special needs are catered for, such as pronounced learning difficulties or physical disability/impairment, and what specialist services, such as specialist tuition or physiotherapy, are provided. Information about a particular school will be supplied automatically to the parent or young person offered a place there, but should normally be given to anyone else requesting it.

Our own investigations and those of other researchers indicate that while some schools put a lot of effort into making their handbooks interesting and attractive for parents to read, there was still much room for improvement in the handbooks of many other schools. One shortcoming in the handbooks of ordinary schools was the failure to give an indication of arrangements or facilities for pupils with special educational needs. Because the range of special needs may be large and change over time, it may be difficult to put this sort of information into the handbook. Handbooks could nonetheless include statements of policy or practice by the education authority, for example, circumstances in which children are likely to receive specialist help or support.

---

* For details about the basic legal requirements, see under "Information for Parents" in the SCC's *The Law of the School* (HMSO Books, 1987) and in *Keeping Parents Posted* (HMSO Books, 1989).

Supplementary information

Education authorities must also issue "supplementary information" saying what their general policies or practices are on a whole range of educational matters, such as the curriculum, discipline and examinations, and on their provisions for educating children and young people with special needs. This information may, again, be in booklet form, but it could be in special leaflets, booklet or information sheets instead. For example, *Grampian's* booklet stated:

> "The cornerstone of the [Education] Committee's policy is that special help should be made available, whenever possible, within mainstream schooling. Another key principle is that children should be educated as close to their family home as possible. The committee is in favour of encouraging parents generally to be full and equal partners in the education of their children and this principle applies particularly where the child has special needs". (The guide then outlines the range of services for children with special needs, with emphasis given to the right of parents to be fully involved in decision-taking.)

Similarly, *Tayside's* supplementary information explained:

> "… it is the policy of the authority that, wherever possible, children with special educational needs should have these needs met in primary and secondary schools. It is the aim of the authority to integrate pupils with physical disabilities into their local schools, and facilities such as ramps and/or lifts are becoming increasingly available in both primary and secondary schools …"

Lothian region also indicated that it was revising the booklet for parents on special educational needs to reflect the authority's policy decision that "education services must respond to special needs within integrated settings …" Other authorities relied on the various 'statutory' letters they must send out at the assessment and recording stages for conveying information to parents. Some authorities explained that they preferred face-to-face contact to the written word for conveying information to parents about special needs provision; and clearly talking to parents in this way is likely to be a sensitive means of doing so, but probably only so long as it is backed up with written information to refer to as well. On the whole written information provided by education authorities in this area appeared to be patchy and piecemeal, with the notable exception of the Grampian, Lothian, and Tayside booklets mentioned above. (But check with your authority — it may be that your authority now issues a booklet of its own for parents giving comprehensive information about meeting special educational needs.)

Statutory letters to parents. The education authority must write to parents of children it proposes to assess, explaining the purpose of the assessment and the procedures involved. We found that the quality of these statutory letters was, on the whole, disappointing; many seemed to have been written with little or no regard to the sensitivities of parents receiving them. The letters were usually written in a legalistic or formal style and conveyed a bare minimum of information. The number of letters involved — as many as half a dozen or more — could also leave parents feeling confused. Few parents would get a clear understanding from these letters of their own role in the assessment and recording processes without other sources of information to turn to. Some authorities, aware of these limitations, arranged for the initial statutory letter, inviting children to be assessed, to be delivered personally and explained to parents by a member of staff. Where this is done and parents have a general information handbook on special educational needs to refer to, the statutory letters clearly become less of a problem. But they could be source of stress, confusion or distrust if they are sent with little supporting explanation or fail to remind parents of their role as partners with professional staff. Parents would undoubtedly find these letters more reassuring and meaningful if they were written in plainer and friendlier language, backed up by proper explanations. They should also be linked up with a personal visit by staff, as is the practice in some authorities.

Information from central government

One of the main sources of information for parents about special educational needs is the "brown booklet", *Special Educational Needs: a guide for parents*, issued free by the Scottish Education Department. This provides general information about parents' legal rights, assessment, recording, the Named Person, and provision for school leavers. A check indicated that while most education authorities reported that they automatically supplied the booklet to parents of children who were being assessed, it was by no means clear how widely the booklet was being made available to parents at large through ordinary schools, public libraries and so on. There have also been reports of parents of children with special needs *not* having come across the booklet at all. One authority said that, because the booklet was aimed at parents of "handicapped" pupils, it preferred not to make the booklet more widely available in case parents of children with less serious difficulties "reacted negatively".

Three other important sources of information, relating to individual children are:

Progress records*

Progress record must be kept on pupils at school, giving details about how well they are each doing in schoolwork, any difficulties on behaviour problems they are having, their school attendance, with reasons for any exclusions ("suspensions") from school, the results of any psychological tests and certain other personal details. The record may also contain other information about a pupil, such as marks awarded in school tests or examinations. The progress record is a confidential document intended mainly for the use of education authority and school staff, and it should not normally be shown to anybody else. Parents have not, in the past, been legally entitled to see their child's progress record, although the law reflecting the practice of some education authorities, could possibly be changed in the near future to allow parents to do so.** Such a right would not only enable parents to check, update or correct the record for inaccurate or misleading information but would also widen the doors to more open communication and goodwill between parents and school staff.

School reports. As a matter of good practice, schools normally issue to parents, at least once a year, a report saying how well their child is doing in different school activities and subjects and describing their child's attitude to schoolwork, behaviour in class, relationships with staff and other pupils, and so on. You should feel free to discuss your child's school report with school staff, and schools may provide parents with special opportunities to do so. Research shows, however, that school reports could be made more informative and helpful to parents — instead of simply containing grades and standard remarks like "poor concentration in class" or "could do better" — and the government was, at the time of writing, looking at ways in which school reports could be improved. One interesting approach is the provision of two-way reports, in which parents are given a report form of their own to fill in about their own observations of how their child is getting on at home. Some special schools make a point of filling in diaries for parents to read each day about their child's progress.

Record of Needs. Parents of children whose special educational needs have been 'recorded' will receive a legal document, the Record of Needs, saying what their child's difficulties and requirements are, and how the education authority will cater for them, together with certain

---

* For more details, see the section on "School records and reports" in *The Law of the School*.
** The government had, at the time of writing, introduced legislation in England and Wales giving parents access to school records on their child, and it is likely that a similar right of access will be extended to parents in Scotland.

other details as described on pages 41-47. It is an important document for parents to refer to when discussing their child's progress or difficulties with school staff, when taking part in reviews of their child's special educational needs (pages 59-60), when discussing their child's future needs beyond school leaving age (pages 61-64) or in any appeals they might make against an education authority's decision (pages 52-58). It is also an important document for parents to have at their side if they have any reason to believe that their child's special educational needs are not being adequately catered for on a day-to-day basis. Parents would certainly be justified in making a complaint to the education authority or, if necessary, taking the matter up with the Secretary of State or going to court if they had reason to believe that the Record of Needs was being ignored or misapplied.

The recording process has nonetheless attracted certain criticisms.

Parents, for example, appear to be given little guidance how to comment on the information which will go into the Record. Since the Named Person is not appointed until the Record is finalised, they may have difficulty in finding someone suitable to turn to for advice. There

is also some concern about the quality or readability of the written information in the Record. Another difficulty is that parents will not necessarily be allowed to see any background reports compiled by specialist staff in drawing up the Record. Parents could find these reports useful should they wish to appeal against a recording decision of something said in the Record (especially if they believe that statements in the Record hide disagreements between staff).

Other sources of information. Apart from the official booklets, letters and documents, referred to above, there are many books about the education of children with learning and other difficulties. Some organisations, such as the Advisory Centre for Education and the Centre for Studies in Integration in Education, have produced a number of publications specially written for parents, although caution should be taken in reading these as not all of them apply to Scotland. A selection of these and useful publications is given at the end of the handbook.

How can assessment and recording processes be improved?

The assessment and recording of special educational needs provides parents with one of their most important opportunities to influence their child's schooling. Parents' views have to be carefully considered in the assessment and recording processes. Despite official guidance and other efforts to promote parental involvement, however, it appears that parents are still not receiving as much information or guidance as they might to make an effective contribution to the assessment and recording processes. This shortcoming is compounded by various others:

- education authorities having different practices about inviting parents along to meetings to discuss the assessment or recording of their child.

- delays in drawing up the Record of Needs, partly due to the backlog of other work, but also due to failure to open the Record immediately after the statutory period for commenting on the draft of the Record has elapsed.

- regional variations in recording practice. The Edinburgh University survey cited above showed that not only were some education authorities more likely to record than others, but also that some authorities recorded certain "areas of need" more frequently than others. For example, the proportion of recorded pupils in 1986 with "cognitive" (general learning) difficulties ranged from 44 to 95 per cent by region or division, and those with social and emotional difficulties from 2 to 57 per cent.

Parents can help these processes to work better by:

- finding out what the education authority's policies or practices are about involving parents in the assessment and recording process — for example by asking for written statements of policy.

- insisting on detailed explanations being given, in writing if necessary, about assessments and the reasoning behind recording decisions.

- asking the education authority for detailed guidance when asked to comment on the information to appear in the Record of Needs.

Ordinary or special school?

The Warnock committee believed that the majority of children with special needs could and should be educated alongside other children in ordinary schools — loosely referred to as "integration" — and it suggested various ways in which this could be done. Children's special educational needs fall along a "continuum", with some children having more requirements than others, so that with goodwill, insight, careful planning and organisation, it should be possible to educate nearly all children with special needs in ordinary schools all or most of the time. There is no justification for assuming that because children have special needs that they must be educated in special schools or that because they attend ordinary schools they have no special needs. A range of special provision can be made within ordinary schooling to match the range of special needs, for example through specialist tuition, adaptations, equipment, auxiliary support and so on. Supportive attitudes of staff and the emotional climate of the school can also help children with special needs to cope with ordinary schooling. At the same time, however, Warnock believed that there would always be some children whose needs were such that they would be best educated at special schools, although not necessarily all of the time or throughout their schooling.

Opportunity for a choice of ordinary or special school

In Scotland the education authority will decide whether to offer your child a place at an ordinary or a special school, but the authority must give you opportunity to ask for and, if necessary, appeal for a school of your own choice, as explained on pages 35-40. The authority's decision will be influenced or determined by:

- its own policies and provisions for educating children with recorded special needs in ordinary schools.

- recommendations arising from any assessments carried out on your child.

- the weight it attaches to your own preferences, including any "placing request" you might make for your own choice of school.

- the results of any appeals you might make, including a decision by the Secretary of State or the court about the school your child should go to.

In England and Wales, the position is somewhat different. There the local education authority must make sure that children with a "statement" of special needs are educated alongside other children in ordinary schools as far as possible. This duty to integrate children into ordinary schooling in England and Wales has less force than at first might appear, however. Integration need not take place if attendance at an ordinary school would be incompatible with the child's special educational needs, interfere with the efficient education of other pupils there or involve the inefficient use of staff or other resources. The law in England and Wales nonetheless lays down a principle not found in the Scottish legislation, which places greater emphasis on parental choice of school to secure integration.

Education in ordinary schools

A number of arguments have been put forward for educating children with special needs in ordinary rather than in special schools:

- *Children with or without special needs should not, for good educational and social reasons, be treated as two distinctive groups for whom separate schools should be provided, a view shared by the Warnock Committee.*

Children with special needs, learn and develop best when in contact with their ordinary classmates all or most of the time, and "even for children with profound learning difficulties, the friendship and society or other children can effectively stimulate learning development."

- *Allowing children with special needs, however severe or complex, to go to ordinary schools also brings about proper social mixing and greater tolerance and understanding of individual differences.* The parliamentary select committee on the working of the English act reported that in Danish and Swedish secondary schools with a maximum commitment to integration there were no indications that educational standards had suffered as a result. As more and more ordinary schools come to regard the education of children with special needs as part of their everyday task, many traditional assumptions and prejudices about "handicapped" children would be expected to disappear.

- *There are good practical reasons for wanting to see pupils with special needs educated in ordinary schools.* Pupils will not usually have so far to travel to and from school; they may have brothers and sisters attending ordinary school; and they will be educated alongside children whose homes are not far away from their own.

Education in special schools

The Warnock committee nonetheless saw a continuing need for special schools to be provided for three groups of children:

- "Children with severe or complex physical, or sensory or intellectual disabilities who require special facilities, teaching methods or expertise which it should be impracticable to provide in ordinary schools.

- "Children with severe emotional or behavioural disorders who have very great difficulty in forming relationships with others or whose behaviour is so extreme or unpredictable that it causes severe disruption in an ordinary school or inhibits the educational progress of other children there.

- "Children with less severe disabilities, often in combination, who despite special help do not perform well in an ordinary school and are more likely to thrive in the more intimate communal and eductional setting of special school". (p.86, para 6.10)

In Scotland there are about 10,000 children in special schools and classes, representing about 1.2 per cent of all children of school age.* Classes are a lot smaller than in ordinary schools.** The vast majority of special schools are for pupils with mild to severe learning difficulties (who represent well over four fifths of all children in special schools). Other special schools are mainly for blind or deaf children, children with cerebral palsy, and children with social and emotional difficulties.

From a parent's point of view, special schools and classes offer certain attractions:

- the smaller classes and intimate atmosphere in special schools allow children to get a lot of individual attention and support from staff.

- staff in special schools are likely to have been specially trained to deal with their child's particular difficulties, such as tuition for very slow learners or children with hearing difficulties.

- equipment and facilities, and perhaps the physical layout of the school, may allow children to cope well in ordinary everyday tasks, such as moving about, toileting, eating and so on.

- services for the child's medical, physical or social welfare, such as auxiliary help, therapy, counselling, and so on, are more likely to be readily available.

Combining the best of both worlds

The Warnock report recommended that ordinary and special schools could work together by:

- sharing or exchanging teaching and other staff for specialist activities, such as arranging for special school staff to spend some of their time conducting special classes in ordinary schools or providing individual tuition in ordinary classes.

- jointly planning timetables and what they teach, so that pupils with special needs can easily move between ordinary and special schools or classes in the course of the school day or week.

---

* "Special Schools," Statistical Bulletin, March 1984, Scottish Education Department. Figures quoted are for 1982.

** Under the conditions of service for teachers in special schools or units, the normal maximum class sizes are: 10 (pupils with moderate or profound learning difficulties); 8 (pupils with severe physical and learning difficulties); and 6 (pupils with visual impairments, hearing loss or communication difficulties; pupils with serious social and emotional difficulties).

- organising more joint educational, social and recreational activities, such as combined school trips, parents' meetings, fund-raising events, extra-curricular activities and so on.

- sharing facilities and equipment, such as school workshops, laboratories, dining halls, gymnasia, playgrounds, libraries and so on.

Ideally links are best developed where special and ordinary schools are close enough to one another. Where this is not possible, the Warnock report suggested that special schools could function as "centres of specialist expertise and research", providing information, advice and expert help for schools, parents, and teacher training. One interesting approach is the provision of an "integration facilitator" who "sits alongside" the child, as it were, to help him or her to take part as fully as possible in the life of an ordinary school.

Current policy and practice

The Edinburgh University study, mentioned above, has indicated that the great majority of recorded pupils continue to be sent to special school (1986 data), with only 18 per cent after assessment and recording attending "mainstream" school and 87 per cent with general learning difficulties going to special school. About 15 per cent of all recorded pupils attended a special class or unit in ordinary school. Only 1.5 per cent attended mainstream school on a "part time" basis. The research team thus concluded:

"Currently, for whatever reason, assessment seems to be associated with the concept of removal from the mainstream rather than centred on the individual special needs of pupils. The Warnock aim of additional or supplementary provision to meet special educational needs in mainstream provision wherever possible rather than distinctive provision for those seen as handicapped does not seem to have been realised in most of the regions or divisions in Scotland."

This study also noted wide regional variations in whether a pupil, after assessment, was attending a special or an ordinary school. This varied by region from 5 to 30 per cent or more of recorded pupils in ordinary schools and from 20 to over 80 per cent in non-residential special schools. The researchers comment:

"It seems reasonable to suggest that these placement patterns are related to an individual recording policy in each area, given that different patterns of recording have evolved from a standard piece of legislation and standard guidelines. Also, pre-existing special provision may affect placement patterns as may variations in the recorded population itself. Alternatively, the variations could be due to pupils being recorded because they attend or are to attend a particular type of provision and the authority will record pupils in that setting."

Positive results have nonetheless started to emerge from some schools in Scotland where integration is being put into practice. A 1987 study of eight primary schools in four different education authorities indicated that "mainstream educators with no 'special' training other than that provided for the teaching of infants report that they can and do offer a positive and accommodating service to the full range of children with special needs."* The majority of staff interviewed saw "social gains" as the most important gain for children with special educational needs, including the development of personal identity, learning to make relationships, developing a system of values and general preparation for life in the community after school. The study, at the same time, reported considerable diversity in the definition and practice of integration and found that in only one of the eight schools were the goals of integration written down anywhere.

The parliamentary select committee which examined the working of the law in England and Wales recommended that more guidance should be given to education authorities for achieving different forms of integration, in ways which preserved the strengths of special schools, as opposed to policies based on widespread closures of special schools.

* "The Process and Practice of Integration" and "A Study of Educator's Viewpoints on Integration", summary reports by Dr Cyril Hellier, Senior Educational Psychologist, Tayside Region, July 1987.

How can arrangements for appointing the Named Person be improved?

The education authority must appoint a Named Person that the parents of recorded pupils can turn to for advice and information, except when the parents opted to do without a Named Person. Written guidance from the Scottish Education Department suggests how the Named Person should be appointed and what his or her main duties are. The appointment of a Named Person was recommended in the Warnock report and the idea has been welcomed in most quarters. Provision of a Named Person has nonetheless attracted a number of criticisms:

- The Named Person is appointed only for parents of children and young people with a Record of Needs (who represent about 2 per cent of pupils) and not, contrary to what Warnock had recommended, for all other parents of children and young people having or likely to have special educational needs, (who represent about another 18 per cent or more of pupils). As many of these pupils without a Record of Needs may still have difficulties coping with schooling, their parents may be in need of as much advice and support as those of recorded pupils.

- The Named Person is not officially appointed until the Record of Needs has been drawn up and finalised. Parents are without a Named Person to turn to for advice and support during the assessment and recording processes.

- Although the Named Person should be somebody acceptable to the parents or young person, such as a trusted friend or professional worker, parents do not have a legal right to choose their own Named Person or appeal against the education authority's choice.

- The legal rights and duties of the Named Person are not as strong or specific as they might be. The Named Person is not automatically entitled to a copy of the Record of Needs except by asking for his or her own copy, nor need the Named Person be informed about any alterations, disclosures or alterations of the Record or the Record being discontinued. The Named Person is not under any legal obligation to become involved in any appeals, reviews or future needs assessments, and need not be informed that these are taking place. An important counter-argument against giving the Named Person legal duties, however, is that he or she is a volunteer, not a paid official.

- The role of the Named Person is not as well defined as some people think it should be. The Named Person is given a lot of discretion to carry out his or her task as he or she thinks fit. Some will limit themselves to providing advice and information, while others may see themselves as an "advocate" representing parents or young people at appeal hearings and other dealings with the authority. A lot may also depend on what training they have received for this role (there is no legal obligation to provide special training, although at least one college of education in Scotland is known to run its own course). It is not clear what role the Named Person should play if he or she has a professional obligation to give first consideration to the needs of the child and this conflicts with the wishes of the parent (e.g. concerning choice of school).

What Support is there for parents of children under school age with special needs?

Education authorities are under a general duty to promote the early discovery and assessment of children with special educational needs — that is from birth, not simply during early schooling. Education authorities are left to decide how this should be done. Their main role here is likely to be encouraging medical, social work and other staff to draw their attention to any children likely to have special difficulties with their education as a result of their medical or other condition. Nevertheless various reports suggest that not enough is being done to raise parental awareness as well.

Parents also report confusion about or unawareness of the multiplicity of agencies (education, health, social work, etc.) which may be in a position to provide their child with support before compulsory school age. Parents may be uncertain, too, about the support they themselves are expected to provide for their child at home.

According to the parliamentary report on provision in England and Wales, parents are also not always being informed about voluntary organisations which might be able to give them support at this stage.

Possible ways round these difficulties are:

- publication of information and advice for parents of children who may have special educational needs, giving guidance about who to approach for further advice about getting children assessed and explaining the role of the various agencies likely to be involved with their child.

- putting parents in close touch with local voluntary organisations, playgroups, and nurseries which could offer advice, information, and support in the pre-school years. Parents could also be encouraged to form their own self-help groups.

How can provision be improved for young people after school leaving age?

Working out a youngster's future on approaching school leaving age is arguably the most difficult stage in education, more so if he or she has special educational needs. A number of key decisions have to be made about:

- whether to continue with full-time education after 16, start full-time employment, combine part-time education with part-time employment, join the Youth Training Scheme (or similar scheme), or go to an Adult Training Centre, and so on

- which courses of full or part-time education to follow. Ones leading directly to employment, to more advanced courses of education (such as degree courses), for extending social and life skills, or ones simply making up for lost schooling?

- which institutions to attend to follow a particular course. Staying on at school, going to college, doing a correspondence course, attending day release classes and so on?

For youngsters with special needs, a number of difficulties may stand in the way of following the course or career they would like:

- The Record of Needs is discontinued once a young person leaves school, so that there is no guarantee that the special help he or she has had during school education will be provided in further education as well. Special needs will only continue to be recorded for young people at school, not if they move to college.

- The Record of Needs is discontinued once the age of 18 is reached, even though there may be a continuing need for special educational provision well into adulthood, with evidence that young adults may not reach their full potential until age 25 or more.

- Apart from careers advice staff and, possibly, their own parents, young people may have few people to turn to for guidance and support in dealings with the education system once they have left school. The person who could help, the Named Person, is only bound to give advice and information as long as the young person continues to be recorded. The Warnock report recommended that a Named Person or another professional contact should be appointed for all young people with special needs during the change from school to adult life.

- Colleges and other institutions offering further education may lack the facilities, support services, specialist adaptations and staff suitably trained for educating young people with special needs. Increased recognition is, however, being given to education for special needs in further education colleges, which are now starting to employ specialist staff and make other arrangements. A voluntary organisation, the Scottish Centre for the Tuition of the Disabled, also provides support for young people and adults with special needs through its regional network of volunteer workers, who give information and advice about learning opportunities; although its main aim is to encourage integration in education after school, the centre also provides home-based tuition in various activities as well.

What about the role of voluntary organisations?

Voluntary organisations have played a leading role in pioneering education for children with special needs, some, for example, running their own special schools for children who are blind or deaf or who have cerebral palsy. The Warnock report saw voluntary organisations increasing their role of communicating "information to parents about the children's special needs" and improving "arrangements for self help and community support for parents" (para 17.8).

The particular strengths of voluntary organisations lie in:

- promoting or developing new approaches to teaching or learning in this area of concern — for example by running schools of their own, or influencing school practices.

- offering advice, information or support to parents or pupils and/or representing them in dealings with the education system.

- offering practical help or support to school or education authority staff — for example in the selection of specialist equipment, provision of holiday schemes, and so on.

- influencing national or local government policies through campaigning, lobbying and other pressure group activities.

Scottish survey finding

Our own investigations among 16 national and 79 regional organisations concerned with disability in Scotland indicated that only a limited number — 24 out of the 39 who replied — said that they had dealings with parents or the educational system in some way. These 24 bodies (including 8 national ones) were mainly concerned with blind, deaf, dyslexic and mentally handicapped children, or children with conditions such as cerebral palsy and spina bifida. Nineteen of them said that they provided information, advice, counselling, meetings, home visits, or practical help for parents. Sixteen were in contact with special schools and 10 had dealings with mainstream schools — for example, advising schools on specialist equipment. Seven said that they were represented on various educational bodies or working parties. Eight had made representations to national or local government about various educational matters. A few had given evidence to the Warnock committee or made submissions on changes in legislation.

Voluntary organisations also provide an important source of feedback from the parents they are in contact with. For example, some organisations drew our attention to the difficulties parents were having in getting the information or advice they needed, in knowing what questions to ask professional staff, or in convincing authority that their children needed more help. One organisation wrote:

"Often in the field of deaf education parents are given insufficient information from education authorities to enable them to make an informed choice as to the educational methods best suited to their child."

Some organisations were perturbed by the limited consultation or involvement in meetings or decisions, for example, one organisation thought that:

"Professional people find it difficult to treat parents as partners, to offer information, to consult parents — and some parents find it difficult to get used to being consulted."

Organisations concerned with problems which normally go unrecorded, such as dyslexia and hyperactivity, reported that parents had special difficulty in making their influence felt:

> "Each parent in this division has to drive hard against the odds in an effort to obtain help for their child. Dyslexia, however severe, is not seen as a reason for recording special needs. The child's difficulties are often not understood by teachers. Only infrequent remedial help is available, and any provision is often too little or too late."

> "It is extremely difficult for parents to get schools to accept that their child's hyperactivity is not simply bad behaviour. Our members are angered at not being told about meetings to discuss their child's problems or about reports being written on their child without their knowledge. When parents are allowed to express their views they are made to feel a bit of a nuisance."

On the other hand, some organisations has some very positive things to say about educational services. A spina bifida group, for example, remarked:

> "In this authority, the education service has been very helpful. Adaptations to schools have not been difficult to obtain. Home teaching is provided whenever the pupil's medical condition requires this."

This group added:

> "In a statutory sense, these are relatively early days for parental involvement. It takes parents a while to understand what is available and to appreciate, in some cases, that they are being encouraged to speak out. Here our branch has contact with the membership in such a way that many difficulties are resolved without them in any way becoming dramas!"

A few organisations wanted to see improvements in the way the Named Person was appointed, in parental access to background reports on their child, in screening processes for the early discovery of difficulties, in the provision of special support for parents in the early years of childhood and in guidance for young people after leaving school.

The above replies suggest that voluntary organisations can, and sometimes do, make a major contribution in providing advice, information, support and practical help for parents and schools alike, but that many nonetheless remain an untapped or under-used resource. Education authorities could possibly do more to encourage parents to contact voluntary organisations in their area.

Schooling: how satisfied are parents?

For parents the main hallmark of how satisfactory education services are is the happiness and progress of their child at school. However well or badly the legal and administrative arrangements for educating pupils with special needs appears to be working, parents will usually judge the education system by their own observations and impressions of the schooling of their own child, rather than what policy statements or official procedures lay down. Parents of pupils with special needs will be particularly concerned that their child is given a good start and that the school is providing adequate specialist support.

Our own survey of parents of children with disabilities, contacted through voluntary organisations, indicated that a majority were very or fairly satisfied with the schooling and the special help their children were getting. Parents of recorded children (51 out of 67) were rather more satisfied than parents of unrecorded children (30 out of 58). A more representative picture should be obtained, however, when the findings of the major study investigation being carried out by Edinburgh University for the Scottish Education Department become available. In the meantime, we reproduce some of the comments made by parents in our own enquiry:

The satisfied parents had a lot of positive things to say about their child's schooling:

> "The school has been absolutely great since our son started there about a year ago. With therapy, he moves and talks a lot more." (Parent of a recorded child with cerebral palsy at a special school.)

> "I have no complaints at all about the school. The staff are most friendly, the atmosphere is good. The children are very well catered for, with therapy, special equipment and a school social worker." (Parent of a recorded child with speech difficulties at an ordinary school.)

Dissatisfied parents

The dissatisfied parents (12 parents of recorded pupils, 28 parents of unrecorded pupils) were mainly concerned about the amount of therapy or special tuition being given or the school not being well enough adapted to cope with their child's difficulties, as in the following comments:

"Our daughter receives occupational, physiotherapy and speech therapy but we would like to see swimming and music therapy, provided as well." (Parent of a recorded child with several disabilities at a special school.)

"We are satisfied with the adaptations and therapy but not with the specialist tuition. Our son could do much better at school but is easily distracted, as most of the children he is with are mentally or socially disturbed." (Parent of a recorded child in wheelchair at a special school.)

"I was quite satisfied with my child's education at primary school but a lot of things at secondary school need sorting out, such as adaptations to school lifts, toilets, entrances, etc." (Parent of a recorded child in wheelchair at an ordinary school.)

"Speech therapy is given only once a week, which isn't really enough. The speech therapist, in asking for more time, is frightened of treading on the teacher's toes."* (Parent of a recorded child in a special unit at an ordinary school.)

"Our son has hand and eye co-ordination problems and as yet cannot write properly. We feel that he desperately needs additional time with the teacher, ideally one-to-one teaching." (Parent of a recorded child at an ordinary school.)

"Our main worry is not about the education our child is getting but with supervision problems at playtimes." (Parent a of recorded partially sighted child in a special unit at an ordinary school.)

"More money is needed to buy more items of equipment and staffing levels at my child's school." (Parent of an unrecorded child with mobility problems at an ordinary school.)

"More flexibility needed with timetabling of subjects. Because of physical disability, my child has to start lessons later or finish them earlier to fit in with therapy sessions." (Parent of an unrecorded child in wheelchair at an ordinary school.)

One parent complained that:

"Our child is taken on too many bus journeys. These are alright for the children who live in the town where the special unit is, but most children travel 20 miles or more to the unit. It is a case of being lifted from a taxi onto a bus, then in the afternoon from a bus to a taxi home. It is exhausting for a child who has to sit in the same position all the time."

It is clear from these replies, then, that while a majority of parents are satisfied with their child's schooling, a number of parents thought that services could be a lot better, particularly if their child was not getting enough specialist support. It is also possible that some of the "satisfied" parents were expressing contentment with a situation which, while not ideal, could be a lot worse.

Home-school links

On the school's links with parents, respondents were on the whole quite satisfied, but some of the replies pointed to a breakdown in communication between home and school. Parents of "recorded" children reported being "very" or "fairly satisfied" with the amount of contact they had with staff and opportunities to discuss their child's difficulties (62 out of 68 replies), the great majority having children at special schools. Parents of children with difficulties which were not recorded were again largely satisfied with the level of contact with staff (42 out of 56). Typical were the following sorts of comments:

"Staff very approachable"

"always made to feel welcome at the school"

"teachers are very sympathetic"

One parent with a child at special school wrote:

> "We have a school-home book in which the teacher writes to us about our child's activities throughout the day. We do the same for the teacher in the evening."

The few dissatisfied parents said that teachers were not always available at the times parents wanted to see them or that they felt under pressure (self-imposed?) not to take up too much of the teachers' time. One parent of a child in a wheelchair at ordinary school complained:

> "We have great difficulty in convincing the teacher that we often know what is best for our child."

Another distressed parent of an unrecorded child wrote:

> "Eight months after my child had moved to secondary school, the teachers were still not aware that he was spastic and had dyslexia. They had not read his medical or educational reports from the primary school. I am very distressed about this and feel that parents are not sufficiently involved."

There are a number of ways in which parents can become more involved in their child's schooling:

- making appointments with individual members of staff to discuss their child's progress (schools will often make special arrangements for parents to meet staff without necessarily waiting for parents to take the initiative).
- attending meetings organised by the school or the parent teacher or parents' association (about half of all schools have a PTA or PA).
- becoming involved in wider issues affecting children's education, such as the funding and staffing of schools, by making their views known to members of their school board, local councillors, members of parliament, government ministers, and so on.

Part Four: Selected Reading List

Selected reading list

Compiled with the assistance of Elizabeth Wallis, Advisory Centre for Education and formerly of the Centre for Studies in Integration in Education.

The reading list below has been drawn up to:

- develop parents' understanding of their own child's difficulties and educational requirements.

- promote parents' awareness of some of the wider issues affecting provision for special educational needs.

- acquaint parents with some of the latest thinking or research on the education of children with special needs.

The publications listed below represent but a small cross-section of the ones available but they can signpost readers to further publications or sources of help. Many of the voluntary and other organisations listed at the end of this handbook also publish booklets, leaflets, newsletters and other materials which may be of interest. You should be able to borrow most of the publications listed here through your local library — even if they are not stocked there, the library can arrange for you to obtain your copy through the inter-library loans service.

General
Advisory Centre for Education, *Special Education Handbook*, second edition 1986.
Detailed commentary on the legislation for England and Wales, but containing useful information and ideas for parents in Scotland. See also ACE's *Summary of Warnock Report, Under 5s with Special Needs* and *Where* reports, nos:

173 (Nov/Dec 1981), "Wider definition of handicap called for in new Open University course."

176 (Mar 1982), "Special Needs: will attitudes change?"

183 (Nov/Dec 1982), "Assessing special needs: parental involvement."

189 (Jun 1983), "Advocacy for special needs."

Len Barton and Sally Tomlinson (eds), *Special Education: policy, practices and social issues,* Harper and Row, 1981.

Consequences of designating more and more children in need of special education. Critical studies of assessment, behaviour modification in special education, educational psychology, role of parents in special education. Maladjustment and local authority decision making. Exclusion of children with special needs from ordinary school.

Len Barton, *The Politics of Special Educational Needs,* The Palmer Press, 1988.

Examines special educational needs and their relation to contemporary society. Topics include the question of special education and ethnic minorities, the role of parents, the Scottish experience and other related issues.

Tony Booth and Will Swann, *Including Pupils with Disabilities,* Open University Press, 1987.

Shows how the participation of children and young people with physical, mental and sensory disabilities in mainstream education and social life can be enhanced, such as the sharing a common curriculum which is at the same time adapted to needs.

Tony Booth and June Statham (eds), *The Nature of Special Education: people, places and change,* Croom Helm, 1986.

Case studies of individuals with disabilities; perspectives by teachers, professionals and those with disabilities, changes in curriculum and administration.

Wilfred Brennan, *Changing Special Education Now,* Open University Press, 1987.

Examines the impact of legislation upon administration and upon schools, the pupils and their parents. Looks at the intentions of the Warnock Report and the various ways education authorities have implemented the 1981 Education Act for England and Wales, but of relevance to Scottish readers as well.

Ted Cole, *Residential Special Education,* Open University Press, 1986.

Range of provision. Who should board? A residential or home-based approach? Parent training and support. Fostering, Intermediate treatment. Contrasting approaches to residential schooling. Curricular issues. Standards of care. Partnership with the family. The case for the special boarding school.

Janet Cross, *Parental Responses to and involvement in the Production of their Child's Record of Needs*, 2 Hillneuk Avenue, Bearsden, Glasgow, 1987.

Summary of a survey among parents from four special schools in Scotland about their experience of the recording process.

Ann Darnborough and Derek Kinrade, *Directory for Disabled People: a handbook of information and opportunities*, Woodhead-Faulkner Ltd in association with the Royal Association for Disability and Rehabilitation, 4th ed. 1985.

Covers the statutory services, financial benefits and allowances, specialised aids and equipment, the house and home, education, employment, motoring and leisure pursuits. Names and addresses of suppliers, and descriptions of the products and services provided are given throughout the text.

Department of Education and Science, Scottish Education Department, Welsh Office, *Special Educational Needs*, (the Warnock report) Cmnd 7212, HMSO, 1978. Committee of enquiry set up to review and recommend policies for the education of children and young people with special needs. Essential background reading. Gives a wide overview of past and present provisions, and wide ranging recommendations for future provision.

W. B. Dockrell, W. R. Dunn, A. Milne (eds), *Special Education in Scotland*, Scottish Council for Research in Education, 1978.

Developments since 1950. Integration of mentally handicapped pupils in secondary school. Maladjusted children. Teacher training. Parental involvement. Curriculum. Child Guidance services. Future development.

J. Fish, *Special Education: the way ahead*, Open University Press, 1985.

Helpful summary of new thinking about and approaches to special education, range of help (including before and after school), assessment, peripatetic (visiting) staff, partnership with parents, and future priorities.

Caroline Gipps, Harriet Gross and Harvey Golstein, *Warnock's Eighteen Per Cent: children with special needs in primary schools*, Falmer Press, 1987.

Identifying and providing for children with learning difficulties in mainstream primary schools.

Harriet Gross and Caroline Gipps, *Supporting Warnock's Eighteen Per Cent: six case studies*, Falmer Press, 1987.

Through detailed case studies the book describes the method of identification of and provision for children with remedial/special needs in primary schools and the impact on the children involved.

Mary H. Hope, *Micros for Children with Special Needs*, Souvenir Press (E. & A.) Ltd., 1987.

Explains what micros can and cannot do. What age to start. Describes some ways of using micros to help with particular difficulties. Where to get help and advice.

House of Commons Third Report from the Education, Science and Arts Committee Session 1986-87, *Special Educational Needs: implementation of the Education Act 1981*, HMSO, 1987.
Volume 1 Together with Proceedings of the Committee and Minutes of Evidence.
Volume 2 Appendices.

Although concerned with the working of the legislation for England and Wales, the report is highly relevant to Scottish education as well.

Inner London Education Authority, *Educational Opportunities for All: report of the committee reviewing provision to meet special educational needs* (Fish report), ILEA 1985.

Report and recommendations of a committee looking at help for children and young people with special educational needs in the inner London area but also of considerable interest to UK audiences as well. A key recommendation was that *all* children as far as practicable be educated in ordinary schools.

Geoff Lindsay, *Screening for Children with Special Needs: multidisciplinary approaches*, Croom Helm, 1984.

Chapters on medical screening and surveillance; the role of the health visitor; audiological screening and assessment; the speech therapist and language disorders; a teacher's point of view; the role of the educational psychologist; the social worker's role and the implications of the Education Act 1981.

Roy McConkey and Bob McCormack, *Breaking Barriers: educating people about disability*, Souvenir Press, 1983, Human Horizon series.

Based on pioneering work carried out in Ireland with Community Attitudes to Retarded Adults (CARA) it explores the feelings and inhibitions that underlie public attitudes towards those whose physical or mental disabilities all too often set them apart from their neighbours. Offers a practical programme for educating people about disability.

Gilbert MacKay (ed), *The Named Person*, Department of Special Educational Needs, Jordanhill College of Education. Conference papers examining the role of the Named Person and some of its anomalies. There are also papers on the development of special education in Scotland and the recording process.

Judith Male, Claudia Thompson, *The Educational Implications of Disability*, Royal Association for Disability and Rehabilitation, 1985. Curriculum, physical access, social arrangements, safety, design, aids and equipment, examinations, counselling and pastoral care, liaison with parents and professionals. Implications for 29 disabling conditions. Further reading. Useful names and addresses.

The Open University, *Special Needs in Education*, 1982. Open University course booklets, readings, and case studies, with associated radio and TV programmes. Further information from the Open University, Walton Hall, Milton Keynes, Bucks. Some central libraries stock their own copies of OU course booklets.

Scottish Consumer Council in association with the National Consumer Council, *Keeping Parents Posted: information about children's schooling and other educational matters*, HMSO Books, 1989.

A comprehensive guide for parents about their legal rights to written information about the schooling of their child and other sources of information about educational matters, with many examples of how parents might put this information to good use.

Scottish Consumer Council, *The Law of the School: a parent's guide to education law in Scotland*, HMSO Books 1987.

This guide written especially for parents in Scotland covers a wide spectrum of the law to do with education, including choice of school, the curriculum, examinations, guidance, information for parents, school closures, school rules, and special educational needs. Also lists relevant Acts of Parliament, regulations, government circulars and explains key educational terms. Reading and address lists.

Scottish Education Department, *Special Educational Needs: a guide for parents*. Free booklet available from the Department, education authorities, advice centres, libraries, etc. providing a basic explanation of the assessment and recording of children with special educational needs.

Scottish Education Department, *Special Needs in Education*, Cmnd. 7991, 1979-80, HMSO. White paper describing the changes in the law proposed for Scotland in the wake of the Warnock report on special educational needs and the report by the Scottish inspectorate on pupils with learning difficulties.

Scottish Education Department:
Circular 1074 "Education (Scotland) Act 1981".
Circular 1080 "Education (Scotland) Act 1981: second".
Circular 1083 "Education (Scotland) Record of Needs Regulations".
Circular 1087 "Education (Scotland) Act 1981: Implementation".

Essential reading for anyone wishing to understand in detail the law relating to special educational needs and how education authorities are expected to put it into practice.

Scottish Society for the Mentally Handicapped, *Information for the Named Person*. Booklet about the role of the Named Person, the recording process, appeals and choice of school, with a useful glossary, the language of special educational needs.

Will Swann (ed), *The Practice of Special Education*, Basil Blackwell/Open University Press, 1981.

Disability and the environment (early influences, sociological perspectives, physical handicap, lead pollution), history of special education. Special provision in ordinary schools, for visually impaired, for physically disabled, remedial education, intermediate treatment, post-school education. Parents, children and professionals. Power and policy in special education. Research, theory and practices.

George Thomson, Sarah Dyer, Karen Thomson, *The Practice of Recording*, Department of Education, University of Edinburgh, 1987. Interim report of a major study into the working of the law and local practice in Scotland in the area of special educational needs. This report shows wide variations between education and authorities in their recording practices.

Sally Tomlinson, *A Sociology of Special Education*, Routledge, 1982.

Critical study of the "ideology" of special education and the moral framework within which the professionals — teachers, psychologists, medical staff operate. Considers the social implications of part of the "mass education system" developing separately as "special" instead of "normal".

Phillip Williams (editor), *A Glossary of Special Education Needs*, Open University Press, 1988.

Comprehensive and comprehensible list of words commonly used in connection with special needs children.

Parental involvement

Dorothy Butler, *Cushla and Her Books: the fascinating story of the role of books in the life of a handicapped child*, Penguin Books Ltd., 1987.

Shows how parents can help the development of children with learning difficulties by reading books to them from a very early age.

Centre for Studies in Integration, *Parents and Professionals: what chance for a genuine partnership* (factsheet).

R. J. Cameron, *Portage: pre-schoolers, parents and professionals: ten years of achievement in the UK*, NFER-Nelson, 1986.

Shows how "portage", a system in which parents and professionals work closely together to further children's development, has gained ground in British schools since being "imported" from America in 1976.

Cliff Cunningham and Hilton Davis, *Working with Parents: framework for collaboration*, Open University Press, 1985.

Parent-professional relationships, understanding parents and families, counselling skills, parent participation aimed at specialists working with parents as "experts" on their own children in the assessment and meeting of special needs.

L. Evans, A. Forder, C. Ward and I. Clarke, *Working with Parents of Handicapped Children: a guide to self-help groups and casework with families*, published for Liverpool Personal Service Society by Bedford Square Press/NCVO, 1986.

Describes and evaluates a four year project to provide help for parents of disabled children. The main focus is on self-help groups and how these may be encouraged and guided towards independence.

Barbara Furneaux *Special Parents*, Open University Press, 1988.

Examines the demands made on parents by children with special needs.

Help Starts Here, National Children's Bureau, 1984, 2nd ed.

Helps parents to use existing services and understand legal and voluntary provisions.

Roy Long, *Developing Parental Involvement in Primary Schools*, Macmillan Education, 1986.

Outlines the background to the issues and describes how to organise specific workshop sessions for teachers, with full supporting material.

Peter Mittler and Helen McConachie, *Parents, Professionals and Mentally Handicapped People: approaches to partnership*, Croom Helm, 1984.

Drawing on experience from nine countries, shows how parents and professionals can work together successfully from infancy to adulthood, in the education of those with serious learning difficulties.

Elizabeth Newson and Tony Hipgrave, *Getting Through to Your Handicapped Child: a handbook for parents, foster-parents, teachers and anyone caring for handicapped children*, Cambridge University Press, 1983.

Shows how parents, in partnership with the professionals, can communicate more effectively and so help the development of children with serious learning difficulties.

Christine Orton, *Children with Special Needs: a guide for parents*, Home and School Council, 1985.

Although written for parents in England and Wales, contains advice, ideas and suggestions of interest to Scottish parents about: help for the child — and the parents; education in ordinary or special school, in hospital or at home; and education after 16.

G. Pugh, *Parents as Partners*. National Children's Bureau, 1981.

Describes ten different schemes for giving parents support through groupwork and home visiting schemes and training them to become educators of their own children.

The Portage Early Education Programme, NFER-Nelson, 1987.

A handbook of activity charts and checklists for parents and professionals involved in "Portage" schemes of home education for pre-school children with learning difficulties.

Jeanette Raymond, *Teaching the Child with Special Needs*, Ward Lock educational, 1984.

Although written for teachers, provides parents with practical insight into skill development, self-help skills like undressing, feeding and toilet training and independence skills like shopping, using money, using the telephone, road safety, etc.

Liz Thompson, *Bringing Up a Mentally Handicapped Child: it's not all tears*, Thorsons, 1986, a Life Crisis book.

A personal story of how the Thompson family has coped with having a mentally handicapped son and brother. Covers ante-natal care, birth to five years, school, adult training centres, residential care and the elderly mentally handicapped.

Keith Topping, *Parents as Educators: training parents to teach their children*, Croom Helm, 1986.

Analyses over 600 international English-language research reports on the effectiveness of parent training programmes.

Diana Wells, *Living with an Allergic Child*, Ashgrove Press, 1985.

How a mother learned to cope with her son's multiple allergies and hyperactivity.

Sheila Wolfendale, *Parental Participation in Children's Development and Education*, Gordon and Breach, 1983.

Integration

Advisory Centre for Education, *Where* reports, nos:

170 (Jul 1981) "Give parents a choice of integration"

175 (Feb 1982) "Parents behind US change to integration"

178 (May 1982) "Integration: lessons from abroad"

179 (Jun 1982) "ACE statement on integration"

180 (Jul/Aug 1982) "Working towards integration"

190 (Jul/Aug 1983) "Integration: theory into practice"

193 (Nov/Dec 1983) "Negotiating integration"

ACE Bulletin, No. 6 (Jul/Aug 1985) "Lack of planning thwarts integration".

Tony Booth and Patricia Potts (eds), *Integrating Special Education*, Basil Blackwell, 1983.
Integration policy and practice. Access to mainstream curriculum in secondary schools. Resources for meeting special needs in secondary schools. Support services for primary schools.

W. K. Brennan, *Special Education in Mainsteam Schools: the search for quality*, National Council for Special Education, 1982.

The background to integration, patterns of provision in ordinary schools for all types of disability, developing ordinary school provision and different models of integration.

Centre for Studies on Integration in Education (CSIE).

Integration: the main arguments (free).

Outlines the arguments supporting integration of children with special needs in ordinary school.

Integration Schemes Strengthen Schools: a research study.

Summarises the findings of a three year study carried out by the National Foundation for Educational Research (NFER) on 17 integration schemes in 14 local education authorities in England and Wales. 1983.

Transferring Good Practice

Half of the pupils at Bishopswood Special School in Sonning Common, Oxfordshire are now educated full-time in neighbouring nursery, primary and comprehensive schools. In this evalutaion, the Bishopswood staff conclude that these children with severe learning difficulties are now receiving an appropriate and improved education, with benefits for ordinary schools.

Mainstreaming in Massachusetts

A report on the experience of integration in Massachusetts, which in 1974 introduced its own special education law. 1986.

Integration in Practice — 1, 2, 3

Accounts of integration schemes in various schools, including a comprehensive school which integrates physically disabled pupils, the all-age integration of blind and partially sighted pupils, and integration of young children with a range of learning difficulties. 1986.

See also the *Publications List* and *Selected Reading List* of the CSIE for the titles of other publications.

Seamus Hegarty and Keith Pocklington with Dorothy Lucas, *Integration in Action: case studies in the integration of pupils with special needs*, NFER-Nelson, 1982.

Fourteen detailed case studies of integration programmes in UK, each representing a different approach within a wide range of special needs. The programmes are reviewed from a number of perspectives including their organisation, aims resources and curriculum.

David Galloway, *Schools, Pupils and Special Educational Needs*, Croom Helm, 1987.

Detailed examination of the changes in attitudes, administration, the curriculum and pastoral care that are needed if teachers in ordinary schools are to meet their pupils' special needs successfully.

Ann Hodgson, Louise Clunies-Ross and Seamus Hegarty, *Teaching Pupils with Special Educational Needs in the Ordinary School*, NFER-Nelson, 1984.

Based on research in 70 schools, this study looks closely at the ways in which teachers in ordinary schools are integrating pupils with special educational needs into classes.

Tony Dessent, *Making the Ordinary School Special*, The Falmer Press, 1987.

Describes practical steps which education authorities and schools need to take in order to cater for children with learning and social behavioural difficulties. Based upon the concept of non-segregation rather than the more customary idea of integration.

Flo Longhorn, *A Sensory Curriculum For Very Special People: a practical approach to curriculum planning*, Human Horizon Series, Souvenir Press, 1988.

Outlines a curriculum for each of the senses in turn, using stimuli which can be varied to suit the age of the child or young person. It shows how these can be amalgamated to create a multisensory experience and how this newly developed awareness can be integrated into the rest of the school curriculum.

Barrie Wade and Maggie Moore, *Special Children … Special Needs: provision in ordinary classrooms*, 1987, Robert Royce.

Describes through case studies examples of successful and unsuccessful practices of integration.

Grace Wyatt with Clive Langmead, *Charnwood: a very special place where handicapped and able children can grow together*, Lion Paperback, 1987.

Shows how children with and without disabilities can grow, play and learn together in an environment untouched by labels and restrictions.

Learning difficulties

Hazel Bines, *Redefining Remedial Education*, Croom Helm, 1986.

Examines the development of remedial education across the curriculum. Looks at subject teaching for pupils with learning difficulties and discusses the new advisory and research role of remedial teachers.

Tony Booth, Patricia Potts and Will Swann, *Preventing Difficulties in Learning: curricula for all*, Basil Blackwell in association with the Open University Press, 1987.

Examines learning difficulties in the context of school curricula which reflects the interests, background and abilities of all pupils.

Tony Branwhite, *Designing Special Programmes: a handbook for teachers of children with learning difficulties*, Methuen, 1986.

A step-by-step guide for designing and presenting special educational programmes, including computer assisted ones, for children who have learning difficulties in the ordinary classroom.

Wilfred K. Brennan, *Curriculum for Special Needs*, Open University Press, 1985.

Outlines the need for a sensitive and responsive programme of curriculum design and development and surveys current trends in curriculum practice in both special and ordinary schools.

John Clarke and Kathleen Wrigley, *Humanities and Children with Special Educational Needs in Secondary Schools*, Cassell, 1987.

Offers a philosophical overview of current trends in thinking about humanities teaching and special needs together with a practical guide to school and classroom organisation.

Judith Coupe and Jill Porter, *The Education of Children with Severe Learning Difficulties: bridging the gap between theory and practice*, Croom Helm, 1986.

Emphasis on enabling a child to be capable of setting his own goals and having the necessary flexible adaptive behaviours to achieve them.

Simon Dyson, *Mental Handicap: dilemmas of parent-professional relations*, Croom Helm, 1987.

Examines the problems facing parents of children with serious learning difficulties and the responses of doctors, psychologists and teachers who work with them. The author's own experience of growing up with a brother with such difficulties adds interest.

Barry Franklin (editor), *Learning Disability: dissenting essays*, Falmer Press, 1987.

What precisely is a learning disability? A US perspective on why this category is growing and is now the largest special education category in US public schools.

Leonora Harding, *Learning Disabilities in the Primary Classroom*, Croom Helm, 1986.

Classifies and describes a wide range of difficulties, discusses problems of diagnosis and remedying them and views certain psychological theories and research findings, relating these to practice in primary school age range (but applicable to lower secondary school as well).

Joan Hebden, *She'll Never Do Anything, Dear*, Souvenir Press, 1988.

The story of a mother's fight to help her Down's Syndrome daughter develop into a bright, independent young woman.

Carol Ouvry, *Educating Children with Profound Handicaps*, British Institute of Mental Handicap, 1987.

Discusses issues which form the background for planning the curriculum for pupils with profound and multiple learning difficulties. Based on classroom experience and the results of a survey carried out by the author.

John Sayer, *Secondary Schools for All? strategies for special needs*, Cassell, 1987.

Reviews current developments and policy issues, paying particular attention to the differences between non-segregation and integration, and arguing that special needs can only be met in the context of the whole school and community.

S. Segal, *No Child is Ineducable*, Pergamon, 1967. A pioneering study showing that learning is possible among children with the severest difficulties.

Scottish Education Department, *The Education of Pupils with Learning Difficulties in Primary and Secondary Schools in Scotland*, HMSO, 1978.

A progress report by HM Inspectorate on work in schools, with a call for pupils with learning difficulties to be taught as far as possible by ordinary class and subject teachers. The report also calls for a wider interpretation of "learning difficulties".

Scottish Education Department, *The Education of Mildly Mentally Handicapped Pupils of Secondary School Age in Special Schools and Units in Scotland*, HMSO, 1981.

HMI report covering the work of schools and special units, past and future development. For a summary of this, see SPTC publication below.

Scottish Parent Teacher Council (SPTC) in association with the Scottish Society for the Mentally Handicapped, *Secondary Schooling for the Mildly Mentally Handicapped: a parent-teacher challenge.*

Summarises the main points in HM Inspectors' report (cited above) on the education of children with mild learning difficulties in secondary school, discussion of how teachers and parents can help one another, discussion topics for parent-teacher and parents' associations.

Colin J. Smith, *New Directions in Remedial Education*, the Falmer Press in conjunction with the National Association of Remedial Education, 1985.

Identifies new approaches in the ordinary school. Examines the assumptions which underpin the practice of remedial education.

Paula Tansley and John Panckhurst, *Children with specific learning difficulties*, National Foundation for Educational Research, 1981.

Review of research, including studies of dyslexia. Neurological, perceptual, physical and environmental factors. Reading difficulties. Remedial treatment, assessment and diagnosis.

Adrian Ward, *Scots Law and the Mentally Handicapped*, Scottish Society for the Mentally Handicapped, 1984.

Comprehensive and very readable explanation of the law about the care, education and welfare of mentally handicapped people in Scotland.

Paul Widlake, *How to Reach the Hard to Teach*, Open University Press, 1983.

Shows how secondary schools can and should be more responsive to the needs of slow learners and other non-academic pupils.

Sheila Wolfendale, *Primary Schools and Special Needs: policy, planning and provision*, Cassell, 1987.

Explores ways in which ordinary primary schools can meet the special needs of their pupils and argues that parents, teachers and education authority staff all have a valid part to play in children's development and education.

Hearing difficulties

D. M. C. Dale, *Individualised Integration: studies of deaf and partially hearing children and students in ordinary schools and colleges*, Hodder and Stoughton, 1984.

Study which concludes that "all but a handful" of hearing impaired children can and should be educated in their ordinary local schools and colleges.

Lorraine Fletcher, *Language for Ben: a deaf child's right to sign*, Souvenir Press, 1987.

The story of Ben's integrated education and his parents' fight to allow him sign language and total communication.

Wendy Lynas, *Integrating the Handicapped into Ordinary Schools: a study of hearing-impaired pupils*, Croom Helm, 1986.

Reviews the research on the academic and social integration of hearing-impaired pupils in ordinary schools. Deals with the reactions of normal hearing pupils to deaf pupils in the ordinary school.

George Montgomery, *The Integration and Disintegration of the Deaf in Society*, Scottish Workshop Publications, 1981.

Collection of papers, originating from a joint Scottish, Northumbrian and Yorkshire Workshop, on the subject of integrating deaf persons into society.

Michael Reed, *Educating Hearing Impaired Children in ordinary and special schools*, Open University Press, 1984.

Physical, social and emotional, medical aspects. Discovery and assessment. Hearing aids. Parents as educators. School and post-school education. Useful organisations.

The Royal National Institute for the Deaf, 1985. *The Hearing Impaired Child in Your Class: a guide for teachers in ordinary schools.*

Covers support services, measuring the amount of hearing, implications of hearing loss, hearing aids, lip reading, aiding understanding during lessons at various stages of child's educational life.

Scottish Association for the Deaf, *First Signs of Hearing Impairment, Is Your Child's Hearing Impaired? First Aid in Hearing Aids, Library List* and other publications.

Scottish Education Department, *The Education of Pupils with Severe Hearing Impairment in Special Schools and Units in Scotland: a report by HM Inspectors of Schools*, HMSO, 1987.

The report discusses the meaning of "hearing impairment" and discusses such issues as integration, the curriculum, the future of small special schools, signing, teaching methods and so on.

Jonathan Solity and Shirley Bull, *Special Needs: bridging the curriculum gap*, Open University Press, 1986.

Brings together the major approaches to the curriculum of children with hearing difficulties.

Alec Webster, *Deafness, Development and Literacy*, Methuen, 1986.

Claiming that there are likely to be children with hearing difficulties in every classroom, this book covers the main causes of hearing loss (mild or severe) and its identification, diagnosis and treatment, the impact deafness has on a child's social and linguistic development, and teaching methods.

Alec Webster and John Ellwood, *The Hearing-Impaired Child in the Ordinary School*, Croom Helm, 1985.

A sourcebook of basic facts about the nature, causes and implications of hearing loss, with coverage of the practical aspects of ensuring maximum involvement of the hearing-impaired child in pre-school, nursery, primary and secondary school.

Medical difficulties and disorders

Advisory centre for Education, "Children in hospital: educational rights," *Where*, 185, Feb 1983.

Arthritis and Rheumatism Council, *When a Young Person has Arthritis: a guide for teachers*.

Brittle Bones Society, *Education for Children with Brittle Bones*.

British Diabetic Association, *The Diabetic at School*.

British Epilepsy Association, *Epilepsy: a guide for Teachers* and *Epilepsy: a teachers' handbook*.

Cystic Fibrosis Society, *School Problems of Children with Cystic Fibrosis* and *Your Fibrosis Child at School.*

Department of Education and Science, *Aspects of Special Education: schools for delicate children — special classes in ordinary schools*, HMSO 1972.

Haemophilia Society, *Introduction to Haemophilia: notes for teachers.*

Home and School Council, *The Child with a Medical Problem in Ordinary School.*

National Association for the Welfare of Children in Hospitals, *Children in Hospital: an action guide for parents.*

National Children's Bureau, reading lists on the *Child with Asthma, A Chronic Medical Problem* and *Epilepsy.*

National Eczema Society, *Coping with School, Children's* and *Teenage* information packs.

National Society for Epilepsy, *Epilepsy at School, Children and Young People with Epilepsy* and other leaflets.

Christine Orton, *The Child with a Medical Problem in Ordinary School*, Home and School Council.

Mobility difficulties

Mog Ball, *In Our Own Right: beyond the label of physical disability*, Community Service Volunteers, 1986.

A resource pack on physical disability for schools, further education, staff training and volunteer training. Helps young people to look critically at local services and suggests ways in which they could become involved in community action projects.

Sarah J. George and Brian Hart, *Physical Education for Handicapped Children*, Souvenir Press, 1983.

Outlines the many sports and games that can be played by physically disabled children, including football, hockey, archery, swimming and relay racing. Discusses different types of physical disability and their special problems.

Sylvia B. Howarth, *Effective Integration: physically handicapped children in primary schools*, NFER-Nelson, 1987.

Concentrates mainly on children with significant or severe physical disabilities or conditions, based on detailed study of 50 such disabled children.

Nicola Madge and Meg Fassam, *Ask the Children: experiences of physical disability in the school years*, Batsford, 1982.

A study of reactions to physical disability by children from both special and ordinary schools.

Gillian T. McCarthy, *The Physically Handicapped Child: an interdisciplinary approach to management*, Faber and Faber, 1984.

General chapters on assessment, treatment, education, sexual development and preparation for adulthood. Specific chapters on cerebral palsy, arthogryposis, limb deficiencies, muscular dystrophy, orthotics and rehabilitation engineering.

Philippa Russell, *The Wheelchair Child*, Souvenir Press, 1978.

Causes of physical disablement, help from the hospital and community services, growing up with a disability, mobility side other than wheelchair, the cost of disability, the physical environment, special education, leaving school, personal problems, visual, play and holiday activities.

Scottish Council on Disability, *Access for Disabled: a guidebook*.

Scottish Education Department, *Educational Buildings for Disabled People*, HMSO, 1984.

Emotional and social difficulties

Tony Booth and David Coulby (editors), *Producing and Reducing Disaffection: curricula for all*, Open University Press, 1987.

Provides a detailed exploration of the relationship between the curriculum and pupil disaffection or disenchantment with school.

Tony Dessent, *Making the Ordinary School Special*, Falmer Press, 1987.

Practical steps which education authorities and schools need to take in order to cater for children with learning and behaviour difficulties, who represent the vast majority of children with special educational needs.

Neil Frude and Hugh Gault, *Disruptive Behaviour in Schools*, John Wiley and Sons, 1984.

Explores the diversity of psychological and sociological approaches to disruptive behaviour at school.

David Galloway and Carole Goodwin, *The Education of Disturbed Children: pupils with learning and adjustment difficulties*, Longman, 1987.

Argues that the problems in the education of pupils with learning and adjustment difficulties result from a lack of coherent policies at all educational levels — from the government to the individual school — and maintains that pupils' special needs cannot be seen in isolation from the needs of other pupils.

Malcolm C. Jones, *Behaviour Problems in Handicapped Children: the Beech Tree House Approach*, Souvenir Press, 1983.

Describes the pioneering work of the Beech Tree House special unit designed to help physically disabled children with severe behaviour problems, including violent and self-destructive behaviour.

Denis Mongon and Susan Hart, *Making a Difference: teachers, pupils and behaviour*, Cassell, 1987.

Re-examines approaches to schools towards pupils traditionally described as disaffected, troublesome or disruptive, arguing that a more broadly based approach involving parents, professionals and pupils is needed.

Scottish Education Department, *Truancy and Indiscipline in Schools in Scotland* (Pack report) HMSO, 1977.

Report and recommendations, still largely not implemented, on provisions and policies on truancy and indiscipline at school, including the curriculum, school organisation, sanctions, guidance and the role of the teacher.

Denis Scott, *Helping the Maladjusted Child*, Open University Press, 1982.

Meaning of maladjustment, deprivation of affection, reactions of children to deprivation, counter-measures, maladjustment arising from defective child-parent relationships, unforthcomingness, overdependence, hyperactivity, prevention of maladjustment.

Alison Skinner, *Disaffection from School:* issues and interagency responses, National Youth Bureau (NYB), 1983.

An annotated bibliography and literature review on absenteeism and disruption and on the responses of schools and other agencies to these and allied issues.

Delwyn P. Tattum, *Management of Disruptive Pupil Behaviour in Schools*, John Wiley, 1986.

Argues that a preventive approach to the problem of disruption in school is a more valid response than the crisis management approach, which results in pupils being sent to special units. Stresses the importance of schools managing their own problem pupils and teachers analysing their own classroom management techniques and interpersonal skills.

Keith Topping, *Educational Systems for Disruptive Adolescents*, Croom Helm, 1983.

Reviews all the available research on 21 alternative systems for the education of disruptive adolescents, ranging from the highly expensive residential special schools to low-cost provision at ordinary schools.

Speech and language difficulties

Association for Stammerers, *The Stammering Child at School*. Elizabeth Browning, *I Can't See What You're Saying*, Angel Press, 2nd ed. 1987.

A parent's story of struggle against officialdom to bring up and educate her "aphasic" child who at $3^1/_2$ could neither talk nor understand speech.

Michael Beveridge and Gina Conti-Ramsden, *Children with Language Disabilities*, Open University Press, 1987.

An introduction to the language disorders of the school age child. Deals with the relationship between language disability, poor attainment in literacy and aspects of the school curriculum.

Dorothy M. Jeffree and Roy McConkey, *Let Me Speak*, Souvenir Press, 1978.

Reference manual for teachers and parents of any children who are slow in acquiring language, with games to encourage vocalisation, listening skills, sound imitation, comprehension, naming things, using different parts of speech and sentence formation, talking together and so on.

Roy McConkey and Penny Price, *Let's Talk: learning language in everyday settings*, Souvenir Press, 1986.

Specially designed for the average parent, the seven chapters progress from understanding what talking is all about, through a series of planned activities that encourage communication, understanding, playing together, using new words, forming sentences and extending language beyond the home setting.

Alec Webster and Christine McConnell, *Children with Speech and Language Difficulties*, Cassell, 1987.

Detailed information on all aspects of speech and language difficulty. Surveys of available resources, such as assessment materials, teaching kits and computer software.

Visual impairments

Elizabeth Chapman and Juliet Stone, *Visual Handicaps in the Classroom*, Cassell, 1987.

Cause and effect of visual impairment. Integration of visually impaired pupils into ordinary school. Role of advisory and support services.

M. Jamieson, M. Parlett and K. Bickington, *Towards Integration: a study of blind and partially sighted children in ordinary schools*, National Foundation for Educational Research, 1977.

Berthold Lowenfeld (ed), *The Visually Handicapped Child in School*, Constable, 1974.

Teaching methods, assessment, curriculum, adjustment.

Royal National Institute for the Blind, *Helping Partially Sighted Children in Ordinary Schools: guidelines for teachers.*

George Thomson, Alexander Budge, Marianna Bultjens, Margaret Leet, *Meeting the Special Education Needs of the Visually Impaired*, University of Edinburgh, Department of Education and Moray House College of Education Department of Special Educational Needs, 1985.

Early identification, recording, the Named Person, integration and segregation, parents' perceptions.

Complex or multiple difficulties

A. B. Best, *Steps to Independence: practical guidance on teaching people with mental and sensory handicaps*, British Institute of Mental Handicap, 1987.

Information on how multiple defects effect everyday contact with the world around. Based on the results of a six-year study of people with learning, hearing and visual difficulties.

Peter Evans and Jean Ware, *'Special Care' Provision: the education of children with profound and multiple learning difficulties*, NFER-Nelson, 1987.

Concludes that the group of children in special care units of special schools have exceptional needs which for the most part are not being met.

James Hogg and Judy Sebba, *Profound Retardation and Multiple Impairment:* volume 2, education and therapy, Croom Helm, 1986.

Stating that no person, even with the most severe impairments ineducable, the book describes relevant forms of educational intervention and therapy.

Margaret Griffiths and Philippa Russell, *Working Together with Handicapped Children: guidelines for parents and professionals*, Souvenir Press and National Children's Bureau, 1985.

Fourteen writers examine the principles which must underlie successful support for an individual child, concentrating upon those children with special needs due to some minor or major impairment of brain functioning. The nature, cause and effect of the common handicaps are considered and their needs outlined.

G. B. Simon (ed), *The Next Step on the Ladder: assessment and management of children with multiple handicaps*, British Institute of Mental Handicap, 1986.

Manual for use in teaching self-help skills and communication to children with mental and sensory handicaps up to a developmental age of about four years.

Rosalind Wyman, *Multiply Handicapped Children*, Souvenir Press, 1986, Human Horizon Series.

Advice for parents on caring for children with multiple handicaps. Offers an approach that treats the whole child, using educational techniques that will maximise all residual and latent abilities. Describes the work of the Ealing Family Centre for deaf-blind children.

L. Wing, *Autistic Children: a guide for parents*, Constable, 1980.

Conductive education:

Philippa J. Cottam and Andrew Sutton, *Conductive Education: a system for overcoming motor disorder*, Croom Helm, 1986.

The central tenet of conductive education is that motor disorder need not result in physical disabilities, which are learning difficulties and which can be successfully overcome. The system was developed in the 1940s and 1950s by Andras Peto in Hungary, and the Institute which he founded claims that about 70 per cent of its pupils achieve 'orthofunction', that is the ability to enter the normal setting of school or work without artificial aids, wheelchairs, ramps etc.

George Currie, *Conductive Education: principles and practices — Scottish perspectives*, St Andrew's College of Education, 1988.

Report of a Scottish based project on current developments and practices.

The Conductor A quarterly magazine launched in 1988 covering news of developments in Conductive Education at home and abroad.

The Foundation for Conductive Education, Department of Psychology (SC), PO Box 363, Birmingham B15 2TT.

Education for special needs at and beyond school leaving age

Elizabeth Anderson and Lynda Clarke in collaboration with Bernie Spain, *Disability in Adolescence*, Methuen, 1982.

Reviews the literature and reports on an extensive study of the psychological problems, the quality of social life and the adequacy of the services available to disabled teenagers in the last years at school.

Richard Stowell, *Catching Up: provision for Students with Special Educational Needs in Further and Higher Education*, National Bureau for Handicapped Students, 1987.

Survey of the needs of and provisions for students with special educational needs in further and higher education in England.

Liz Sutherland, *A College Guide: meeting special educational needs in Scotland*, National Bureau for Handicapped Students, 1987.

Describes how further education in Scotland can help students with physical and sensory disabilities, learning and behaviour difficulties.

Journals and reference books

British Education Index, University of Leeds.

Lists and analyses the subject content of all articles of permanent educational interest appearing in a wide range of English language periodicals published in the British Isles, together with certain internationally published periodicals. Over 200 periodicals are scanned. The index is published quarterly with an annual cumulative volume.

British Journal of Special Education, published by The National Council for Special Education, 1 Wood Street, Stratford-upon-Avon, Warwickshire, CV37 6JE, quarterly.

The principle forum for new thinking, research and experiment in special needs provision.

Catalogue of Library Holdings, The National Library for the Handicapped Child, Dixon Gallery, 20 Bedford Way, London WC1L 0AL, 1986.

Established under the sponsorship of the Enid Blyton Trust for Children in 1984 and officially opened in 1985. Currently holds over 5,000 children's books, about 1,000 reference books, many relevant periodicals, some audio visual materials, computers, software and toys. Nothing can be borrowed, but enquiries are encouraged.

Current Awareness Service, British Institute of Mental Handicap, monthly. Wolverhampton Road, Kidderminster, Worcs. DY10 3PP.

Lists all British and American books and periodicals, with a back up photocopy service for selected articles listed in the bibliography. All special needs covered.

Disability Alliance, *Disability Rights Handbook,* current edition.

A guide to the rights, benefits and services for all people with disabilities and their families. Updated regularly.

Encyclopedia of Special Education, John Wiley & Sons Ltd., 1987.

Written by over 300 expert contributors with over 2,000 literature references.

European Journal of Special Needs Education, editor Seamus Hegarty, quarterly John Wiley & Sons Ltd., 1986.

Taking a broad view of special education, the journal includes research studies of theoretical, methodological and practical interest, book reviews and accounts of current practice and current software.

Special Children, editor Howard Sharron, monthly (ten times a year excluding July and August), editorial offices, 6/7 Hockley Hill, Hockley, Birmingham B18 5AA, 1985.

The magazine for those concerned with children who have special educational needs.

Education authority publications of interest to parents of children and young people with spinal educational needs. (Obtainable from the education offices of the regional council concerned).

Dumfries and Galloway Regional Council, *Report of the Working Party on Children with Learning Difficulties* (1983).
Reports and policy recommendations covering assessment and recording procedures, provision for children with profound and severe learning difficulties, remedial education, and provision for disturbed children.

Grampian Regional Council, *Guide to Education Services for Children with Special Needs*. A comprehensive guide to services in Grampian Region, including provision for physical, sensory, language, intellectual and emotional difficulties. Also covers pre-school, remedial, further education and hospital provision.

Lothian Regional Council, *Special Educational Needs: information for parents*. A booklet describing the main legal provisions and the regional council's arrangements for children with special educational needs.

Strathclyde Regional Council, Renfrew Division, *The Child with a Physical Disability at Ordinary School*. A 120-page book for teachers but of interest to parents as well covering the integration of pupils with physical disabilities, neurological impairments, or physical illnesses and other conditions.

Tayside Regional Council, *Pupils with Special Educational Needs: a parent's guide to recording*. Through a series of questions and answers, the guide helps parents understand their child's special educational needs and how they are assessed and recorded and catered for at school.

Part Five: Sources of Further Help

Key Terms Explained

Sources of Further Help: Voluntary and Allied Bodies*

ACTION '81
52 Magnaville Road
Bishops Stortford
Hertfordshire CM23 4DW
Tel: 0279-503244

A national and regional network of parents of children with special educational needs, providing information and support in relation to the 1981 Education Act (England and Wales). *Action 81* leaflet.

ACTION RESEARCH FOR THE CRIPPLED CHILD

Vincent House   54 Port St
North Parade   Stirling FK8 2LJ
Horsham   (0786-71444)
West Sussex RH12 2DA
Tel: (0403) 210406

Supports research into the prevention of crippling diseases or alleviation where this is not possible. Publications, including quarterly *Action Research Magazine* and *Integrating the Disabled*.

ADVISORY CENTRE FOR EDUCATION
18 Victoria Park Square
London E2 9PB
Tel: (01-980-4596)

Advice and information on a wide range of educational matters of parental interest or concern. Bi-monthly *Ace Bulletin*. Handbooks for parents on educational topics, including special educational needs (see *reading list*).

AFASIC-ASSOCIATION FOR ALL SPEECH IMPAIRED CHILDREN

347 Central Market Street   Twenty-four hour
Smithfield   'helpline'
London EC1A 9NW   on 041-637-2262
Tel: 01-236-3632/6487

An Association of parents and professionals concerned with children who suffer from speech and language difficulties. Advice and support given.

---

* Every effort has been made to make this list as comprehensive and up-to-date (March 1988) as possible. Current information is obtainable from the information department of the Scottish Council on Disability, which also publishes its own directory of national and local groups. The names and addresses of Scottish contacts for each body are given where applicable. For names and addresses of official and professional organisations concerned with education, see the companion volumes, *The Law of the School* and *Keeping Parents Posted*.

AIDS TO COMMUNICATION IN EDUCATION
Ace Centre
Ormerod School
Waynflete Road
Headington
Oxford OX3 8DD
Tel: 0865-63508

Advice and information about communication aids in education including the assessment of individual needs. Publications, including *Software and Equipment for Children with Severe Learning Difficulties* and *Communication Aid Programs for the BBC*.

ARTHRITIS AND RHEUMATISM COUNCIL FOR RESEARCH, SCOTTISH OFFICE
29 Forth Street
Edinburgh EH1 3LE
Tel: 031-557-2578

Promotes research into arthritis and other rheumatic diseases. Publications and magazines.

ASSOCIATION FOR CHILDREN WITH HEART DISORDER (SCOTLAND)
11 Millerfield Place
Edinburgh EH9 1LW

Parental support groups. Welfare assistance with hospital visiting.

ASSOCIATION FOR THE EDUCATION & WELFARE OF THE VISUALLY HANDICAPPED
c/o Hon. Secretary
Royal Blind School
Craigmillar Park
Edinburgh EH16 5NA
Tel: 031-667-1100

Promotes teacher training and advises in education of visually handicapped pupils.

ASSOCIATION OF PARENTS OF VACCINE-DAMAGED CHILDREN
2 Church Street
Shipston-on-Stour
Warwickshire
Tel: 0608-61595

Mrs Helen Scott
21 Saughton Mains Garden
Edinburgh EG11 3QG
Tel: 031-443 9287

Support group for parents of children damaged by immunisation.

ASSOCIATION FOR STAMMERERS
c/o The Finsbury Centre
Pine Street
London EC1R 0JH

Secretary:
Andrew Holland
Tel: 01-855-1554

Information, advice, support and self-help groups for stammerers and their families.

ASSOCIATION OF WORKERS OF MALADJUSTED CHILDREN
Harmeny School
Balerno, Midlothian
Tel: 031-449-3938

BRITISH ASSOCIATION OF THE HARD OF HEARING
Mr Christopher Shaw
7/11 Armstrong Road
Acton
London W3 7JL
Tel: 01-743-1110/1353

Mrs Nessie Smith
12/27 Ethel Terrace
Edinburgh EH10 5NA
Tel: 031-447-5332

BRITISH ASSOCIATION OF TEACHERS OF THE DEAF
Aberdeen School for the Deaf
Regent Walk
Aberdeen AB2 1SX
Tel: 0224-480303

Professional association providing information and promoting research and
training in the education of the hearing impaired. Bi-monthly journal. Scottish
committee. Information advice, support, conferences, training on all aspects of
provision for the hearing impaired. Scottish contacts.

BRITISH DIABETIC ASSOCIATION
Scottish contact
8 Hillpark Loan
Edinburgh EH4 7BH
Tel: 031-312-7675

Advice, information and support for diabetics and their families, research,
holiday schemes. Scottish contacts. Publishes a *Schools Pack* for parents and
teachers, bi-monthly *Balance*, and various information sheets. Lists of books,
equipment, videos and other items.

BRITISH DYSLEXIA ASSOCIATION
98 London Road
Reading
Berkshire RG1 5AU
Tel: 0734-668271/2

Information and support for parents. Publications list and leaflets. Journal
Dyslexia Contact Scottish contacts/groups (see under Scottish Dyslexia
Association).

BRITISH HEART FOUNDATION
102 Gloucester Place
London W1H 4DH
Tel: 01-935-0185

16 Chester Street
Edinburgh EH3 7RA
Tel: 031-226 3705

Finances and encourages research into all heart conditions. Provides a series of
leaflets giving advice to patients.

BRITISH INSTITUTE OF MENTAL HANDICAP
Scottish Division
Gogarburn Hospital
Glasgow Road
Edinburgh EH12 9BJ

Runs conferences, training courses and brings together various interests in the area of mental handicap.

BRITISH MIGRAINE ASSOCIATION
178A High Road
Byfleet
Weybridge
Surrey
Tel: 09323 52468

Promotes research into migraines. Newsletter, information and publications.

BRITISH POLIO FELLOWSHIP
Bell Close
West End Road
Ruislip
Middlesex HA4 6LP
Tel: 0895 675515

Personal welfare services: social, recreational and cultural activities provided through branches in Scotland. Holiday accommodation in England.

BRITISH RETINITIS PIGMENTOSA SOCIETY
Greens Norton Court
Greens Norton
Towcaster
Northants NN12 8BS
Tel: 0327-53276

Ms I. Solomons
105 Dundrennan Road
Glasgow G42 9SL
Tel: 041-649-8380

Advice, information, and support and promotion of research. Four Scottish branches. Publications, including Guide to *Retinitis, Pigmentosa, Your Questions Answered* and *Young People with Retinitis Pigmentosa*.

BRITTLE BONE SOCIETY
Unit 4, Block 20
Carlunnie Road
Dunsinane Estate
Dundee DD2 3QT
Tel: 0382-817771

CENTRE ON ENVIRONMENT FOR THE HANDICAPPED
35 Great Smith Street
London W1P 3BJ
Tel: 01-222-7980

Provides specialist technical advice and information on design of buildings for disabled people. Publications, including journal *Design for Special Needs, Access Design Sheet Series* and seminar reports.

CENTRE FOR STUDIES IN INTEGRATION IN EDUCATION
Fourth Floor
415 Edgeware Road
London NW2 6NB
Tel: 01-452-8642

Publications advice (incl. free literature), information, campaigning and research on provisions for integrating children with special needs in ordinary schools. Conferences.

CHALLENGER CHILDREN'S FUND
28-30 Howden Street
Edinburgh EH8 9HW
Tel: 031-668-3371

Provides grants for the maintenance, clothing, education and general benefit of physically disabled children and young people up to the age of 18.

CHEST, HEART AND STROKE ASSOCIATION

Tavistock House North
Tavistock Square
London WC1H 4JE
Tel: 01-387-3012

65 North Castle Street
Edinburgh EH2 3LT
Tel: 031-225-6963

Leaflets on chest, heart & stroke illnesses; welfare fund; research, volunteer stroke schemes throughout Scotland.

CLEFT LIP AND PALATE ASSOCIATION

1 Eastword Gardens
Kenton
Newcastle-upon-Tyne
NE3 3DQ
Tel: 091-2859346

R. Razzell
Dept of Speech Therapy
Royal Hospital for
Sick Children
Rillbank Terrace
Edinburgh

Information, advice, support for families of children with cleft lip and/or palate, promotion and funding of research, annual newsletter and leaflets.

COMMUNICATION AIDS FOR LANGUAGE AND LEARNING (CALL)
University of Edinburgh
4 Buccleuch Place
Edinburgh EH8 9LW
Tel: 031-667-1438

Provision of information, assessment, loans and advice on a wide range of computer-based aids to communication and writing, including their use in educational settings. CALL also develops new hardware and software and carries out research into policy for aids provision.

CYSTIC FIBROSIS RESEARCH TRUST

5 Blyth Road
Bromley
Kent BR1 3RS
Tel: 01-464-7211

39 Hope Street
Glasgow G2 6AE
Tel: 041-226-4244

Information. Parent support group. Fund raising for research.

DIAL-DISABLEMENT INFORMATION AND ADVICELINE SCOTLAND
Braid House Day Centre
Labrador Avenue
Howden East
Livingston
West Lothian EH54 6BU
Tel: 0506-33468

DISABLEMENT INCOME GROUP (DIG)
Ecas House
28-30 Howden Street
Edinburgh EH8 9HW
Tel: 031-667-0249/031-668-3577

Runs welfare benefits counselling service, supports research, and promotes
legal rights and welfare needs arising from disablement. Local branches.

DISFIGUREMENT GUIDANCE CENTRE
52 Crossgate
Cupar
Fife KV15 5WS
Tel: 0337-7281

Confidential information, advice, support and practical help for people with
disfigurement problems through personal, family and telephone services.
Educational projects for primary schools. Workshops, training and seminars for
lay and professional groups. Journal *Deep Skin Bulletin*.

DYSLEXIA INSTITUTE
Dowanhill
74 Victoria Crescent Road
Glasgow G12 9JN
Tel: 041-334-4549

EPILEPSY ASSOCIATION OF SCOTLAND
48 Govan Road
Glasgow G51 1JL
Tel: 041-427-4911

Information and counselling services on epilepsy. Employment and training
facilities. Social and welfare activities. Branches and self-help groups
throughout Scotland.

FAMILY FUND
PO Box 50
York YO1 1UY

A government fund run by the Joseph Rowntree Memorial Trust to help
families of children under 16 with very severe learning difficulties. Help, which
is aimed at complementing and not replacing existing services, includes
provision of laundry equipment, family holidays, outings, driving lessons,
clothing, bedding, recreational and other items. Parents applying should give
details of their child's difficulties and the help required.

FRIEDREICH'S ATAXIA GROUP

Cranleigh Works
The Common
Cranleigh
Surrey GU6 8SB
Tel: 0483-27241

34 Petershill Avenue
Paisley PA2 8BA

Funding of research and information, advice and support to sufferers and their families including group holidays. Issues leaflets, newsletter *FAX* and *Information Pack*.

HAEMOPHILIA SOCIETY

123 Westminster Bridge Road
London SE1 7HR
Tel: 01-928-2020

41 Dick Place
Edinburgh EH9 2JA
Tel: 031-667-8694

Advice, information and support for people with haemophilia, their families and those who care for sufferers. Promotion of research. Publications, including quarterly *Bulletin*.

HEADWAY — NATIONAL HEAD INJURIES ASSOCIATION

200 Mansfield Road
Nottingham NG1 3HX
Chryston
Tel: 0602-622382

11 Barcaldine Avenue,
Glasgow
Tel: 041-779-1723

Self-help and support organisation for patients, relatives and professional workers. Publications list, quarterly *Headway News*, pamphlets and booklets, including *Services to Help the Head injured and their Families*.

HELEN ARKELL DYSLEXIA CENTRE

Trensham
Farnham
Surrey GU10 3BW
Tel: 025-125-2400

Information, advice and tuition centre, conferences, courses, mobile units, links with Scottish Dyslexia Association. Leaflet: *Books and Teaching Aids*.

HYPERACTIVE CHILDREN'S SUPPORT GROUP

71 Whyke Lane
Chichester, Sussex
Tel: P903-75182

Information, advice and support for families. Local groups.

INVALID CHILDREN'S AID NATIONWIDE

198 City Road
London EC1V 2PH
Tel: 01-608-2462

Promotion of welfare of disabled children and young people, family support services, residential schooling, advice and information. Publications list, quarterly Newsletter.

JOINT COMMITTEE ON MOBILITY FOR THE DISABLED
9 Moss Close
Pinner
Middlesex HA5 3AY
Tel: 01-866-7884

Represents the mobility and access interests of disabled people and seeks to influence government policy and legislation. Publishes information sheets.

LADY HOARE TRUST FOR PHYSICALLY DISABLED CHILDREN
7 North Street
Midhurst
West Sussex GU29 9DJ
Tel: 073-081-3696

52 Ibrox Street
Glasgow
Tel: 041-427-0321

Provides financial help towards purchase of special equipment, holidays for disabled children, hospital visits and other needs; family support through its social workers.

LEUKAEMIA CARE SOCIETY
PO Box 82
Exeter
Devon EX2 5DP
Tel: 0392-218514

Rose Eden
Elliot
Arbroath
Angus
Tel: 0241-76214

Provides personal support, counselling and limited financial help to sufferers and families of sufferers with leukaemia and allied blood disorders. Runs own holiday caravans. Publications: newsletter (3 times a year), leaflet and brochure.

MANIC DEPRESSION FELLOWSHIP
c/o Scottish Association for Mental Health
40 Shandwick Place
Edinburgh EH2 4RT

Support and information for sufferers. Video available. Local branches.

MENTAL HEALTH FOUNDATION SCOTLAND
7-15 Dean Bank Lane
Edinburgh EH3 5BS
Tel: 031-332-8773

Finances community care projects and research.

MIGRAINE TRUST
45 Great Ormond Street
London WC1N 3HD
Tel: 01-278-2676

Promotes research and the exchange of information concerning migraine. Publications: *Understanding Migraine* (1982), *Migraine News* (2 issues a year).

MUSCULAR DYSTROPHY GROUP OF GREAT BRITAIN AND NORTHERN IRELAND

Nattrass House
35 Macaulay Road
London SW4 0QP
Tel: 01-720-8055

Room 262
11 Bothwell Street
Glasgow G2
Tel: 041-221-4411

Information, family support, literature and promotion of research. Publishes quarterly magazine *The Search* and monthly newsletter *In Focus.*

NATIONAL ASSOCIATION FOR GIFTED CHILDREN IN SCOTLAND
c/o Breeze, Campbell and Paterson
257 West Campbell Street
Glasgow G2 4TU
Tel: 041-248-5434

Advises on campaigns on and issues information about all aspects of the education of children and young people with special abilities or aptitudes.

NATIONAL ASSOCIATION FOR THE WELFARE OF CHILDREN IN HOSPITAL (SCOTLAND)
15 Smith's Place
Edinburgh EH7 8HT
Tel: 031-553-6553

Promotes the needs of sick children, help parents to prepare for children going into hospital and seeks to ensure that child health services are planned with the special needs of children in mind.

NATIONAL BUREAU FOR STUDENTS
336 Brixton Road
London SW9 7AA
Tel: 01-737-7166

Dr J. Cook
Jordanhill College of Education
76 Southbrae Drive
Glasgow G13 1PP
Tel: 041-989-1232

Information, advice and support for people with disabilities in post-15 education. Publications including *College Guide: meeting special educational needs in Scotland*, journal *Educare*, and a Scottish newsletter.

NATIONAL CHILDREN'S BUREAU
8 Wakeley Street
London EC1V 7Q4E
Tel: 01-278-9441

Mrs Helen Morrison
Achamore Centre
57 Ladyloan Avenue
Glasgow G15 8JR
Tel: 041-944-4766

Information, research, conferences, publications on a wide range of matters affecting the education and welfare of children. Interests include parental involvement in schooling, children 'at risk', and special educational needs.

NATIONAL COUNCIL FOR SPECIAL EDUCATION

1 Wood Street
Stratford-upon-Avon
Warwickshire CV37 6JE
Tel: 0789-205332

"Langdene"
271 Glasgow Road
Dumbarton G82 1EE
Tel: 0398-64476

Information, advice, conferences, training and publications on all aspects of special educational need. Publishers quarterly *British Journal of Special Education*, annual conference reports and *Developing Horizons* series. East, north and west of Scotland branches.

NATIONAL DEAF CHILDREN'S SOCIETY

45 Hereford Road
London W2 5AH
Tel: 01-229-9272

Exists to represent deaf children's interests nationally and locally, and to support parents through a large network of self-help groups. Regional groups in Scotland.

NATIONAL ECZEMA SOCIETY

Tavistock House North
Tavistock Square
London WC1H 9WX
Tel: 01-388-4097

5 Lochmaben Drive
Larbert
Stirlingshire FK5 4UT
Tel: 0324-554-741

Promotes research and public awareness about eczema. Local contacts and groups. Publishes baby, children, teenage and adult information packs and journal *Exchange*.

NATIONAL FEDERATION OF THE BLIND

c/o Terry Moody
27 Kelvinside Terrace South
Glasgow G20 6DW
Tel: 041-946-6796

NATIONAL LIBRARY FOR THE HANDICAPPED CHILD

University of London Institute of Education
20 Bedford Way
London WC1 0AL
Tel: 01-636-1500, ext 598, or, after hours 01-255-1363

NATIONAL PORTAGE ASSOCIATION

Mollie White (Secretary)
King Alfred's College
Sparkford Road
Winchester
Tel: 0962-62281

Promotes home teaching and support for parents of young children with special needs.

PARTIALLY SIGHTED SOCIETY
Queens Road
Doncaster DN1 1NX
Tel: 0302-68998

Offers assistance and support to visually disabled people. Information, advice, special printing and enlarging facilities.

PATIENTS' ASSOCIATION
Room 33
18 Charing Cross Road
London WC2H 0HR

Mrs M. Buchanan
29 Leander Crescent
Renfrew
Tel: 041-885-0001
Mrs J. Hargreaves
1 Sycamore Crescent
Inverness
Tel: 0463-224390

Represents and promotes the interests of patients, offers information and advice, and issues information leaflets.

PHYSICALLY HANDICAPPED AND ABLE-BODIED (PHAB)
Tavistock House North
Tavistock Square
London WC1H 9HX
Tel: 01-388-1963

Ms Carol Downie
Scottish PHAB Office
Princes House
5 Shandwick Place
Edinburgh EH2 4RG
Tel: 031-229-3559

Uses social means (clubs and holidays) to bring physically disabled and able-bodied children and young people together.

PHOBICS SOCIETY
4 Cheltenham Road
Chorlton-cum-Hardy
Manchester M21 1QN

Promotes the relief and rehabilitation of persons suffering from agoraphobia and other phobic conditions. Please send S.A.E.

ROYAL ASSOCIATION FOR DISABILITY AND REHABILITATION (RADAR)
25 Mortimer Street
London W1N 8AB
Tel: 01-637-5400

Provides information on all aspects of daily living for physically disabled people and campaigns for improvements in services and standards. Publications, including *The Educational Implications of Disability*. Publications list also available.

ROYAL NATIONAL INSTITUTE FOR THE BLIND

224 Great Portland Street
London W1N 6AA
Tel: 01-388-1266

9 Viewfield Place
Stirling FK8 1NL
Tel: 0786-51752

The RNIB runs schools, homes, hotels, rehabilitation centres and employment services. Supplies material in braille and moon and on tape. The Scottish branch resource centre stocks equipment for display, sale and trial use and has a recording studio for the student tape libarary. The branch also provides educational careers and other advice (Tel: 041-221-1419).

ROYAL NATIONAL INSTITUTE FOR THE DEAF

105 Gower Street
London WC1E 6AH
Tel: 01-387-8033

9a Claremont Gardens
Glasgow G3 7LW
Tel: 041-332-0343

Advice, information and resources on all aspects of education for the hearing impaired.

SICKLE CELL SOCIETY

Green Lodge
Barretts Green Road
London NW10 7AP
Tel: 01-961-7795

Information, advice and support for parents of children with sickle cell disease.

SCOTTISH ASSOCIATION FOR THE DEAF

Moray House College of Education
Holyrood Road
Edinburgh EH8 8AQ
Tel: 031-556-8137

Responsible for promoting interests and welfare of all deaf people in Scotland and bringing together the work of all statutory bodies and voluntary organisations concerned with deafness. Publications: *Early Signs of Hearing Impairment, Is Your Child Hearing Impaired? The Hearing Impaired Child in Your Class* and several other titles.

CITIZENS ADVICE SCOTLAND

26 George Square
Edinburgh EH8 9LD
Tel: 031-667-0156/7

Provides information and support to citizen's advice bureaux throughout Scotland. Does *not* deal with enquiries from the general public except through local citizens advice bureaux. Comments on matters of social concern. Publications: *Annual Report*, including names, addresses and telephone numbers of local CABx.

SCOTTISH ASSOCIATION FOR MENTAL HEALTH
40 Shandwick Place
Edinburgh EH2 4RT
Tel: 031-225-4446

Information service for anyone involved in mental health matters, support for local groups and pressure group activities.

SCOTTISH CENTRE OF TECHNOLOGY FOR THE COMMUNICATION IMPAIRED
Victoria Infirmary
Langside
Glasgow G42 9TY
Tel: 041-649-4545 ext 5579/5580

SCOTTISH CENTRE FOR THE TUITION OF THE DISABLED
Queen Margaret College
36 Clerwood Terrace
Edinburgh EH12 8TS
Tel: 031-339-5408

Promotes integration of adults with disabilities to existing opportunities for learning and leisure. Provides information and advice about such opportunities to adults through a network of voluntary organisers who visit individual homes. Will also find volunteer tutors to work on a one to one basis with those adults who cannot participate in local opportunities for learning. Activities include craft, leisure and academic pursuits. Information leaflet and regular newsletter (by subscription).

SCOTTISH CHILD AND FAMILY ALLIANCE (SCAFA)
55 Albany Street
Edinburgh EH1 3QY
Tel: 031-557-2781

Promotes the welfare of children and families by developing links between professional and voluntary workers in education, health, law, social work and related areas. Runs conferences and training course. Issues publications, including newsletter. "Contact Scheme" (in Tayside area) for parents of children with special needs.

SCOTTISH CHILD LAW CENTRE
1 Melrose Street (off Queen's Cres.)
Glasgow G4 9BJ
Tel: 041-333-9305

Offers advice to children, parents and professionals on law relating to children and young people up to the age of 18; campaigns for changes in the law and comments on new legislation.

SCOTTISH COUNCIL ON DISABILITY

Princess House
5 Shandwick Place
Edinburgh EH2 4RG
Tel: 031-229-8632

National voluntary organisation for all Scotland's disabled people. Concerned with all types of disability, physical, mental and sensory. Services include a free telephone and letter answering enquiry service, the mobile advice centre, a travelling exhibition of information, aids and equipment. Bi-monthly newsletter.

SCOTTISH COUNCIL FOR SPASTICS

22 Corstorphine Road
Edinburgh EH12 6HP
Tel: 031-337-9876

Plans, initiates, promotes and assists schemes and activities directed towards the well-being of persons suffering from cerebral palsy and allied conditions. The council runs own residential schools, day school, day and work centres, residential homes as well as providing mobile therapeutic and social work services.

SCOTTISH COUNCIL FOR VOLUNTARY ORGANISATIONS

18/19 Claremont Crescent
Edinburgh EH7 4QD
Tel: 031-556-3882

Provides information, training and other support services for wide range of national and local voluntary bodies in Scotland.

SCOTTISH DOWN'S SYNDROME ASSOCIATION

54 Shandwick Place
Edinburgh EH2 7RT
Tel: 031-226-2420

Promotes local parent/child self help groups; supports research into Down's Syndrome; provides counselling; lobbies government other bodies on all aspects of provision.

SCOTTISH DYSLEXIA ASSOCIATION

7 Napier Road
Edinburgh EH10 5AZ

Information, advice and support for parents, teachers and education authorities. Publications list and information leaflets.

SCOTTISH LEARNING DIFFICULTIES ASSOCIATION

53 Craw Road
Paisley PA2 6AE
Tel: 041-889-7540

Promotes the education and welfare of children with learning difficulties and other special educational needs, through the exchange of information and ideas with other bodies having similar aims. Organises national and local conferences. Publishes own newsletter.

SCOTTISH PARENT TEACHER COUNCIL
30 Rutland Square
Edinburgh EH1 2BW
Tel: 031-225-4726

With over 400 member parent-teacher and parents' associations, the SPTC represents and promotes the interests of parents on a wide range of educational issues in dealings with central and local government. Annual conference, seminars, information updates, booklets for parents.

SCOTTISH PRE-SCHOOL PLAYGROUPS ASSOCIATION
16 Sandyford Place
Glasgow G3 7NB
Tel: 041-221-4148

Information, advice and support for parents and other volunteers setting up and running playgroups and mother and toddler groups. Regular newsletters and publications list.

SCOTTISH SOCIETY FOR AUTISTIC CHILDREN
Room 2, 2nd Floor
12 Picardy Place
Edinburgh EH1 3JT
Tel: 031-557-0474

Promotes welfare, education and care of persons diagnosed as autistic or with severe communication problems. Provides support for parents and promotes public knowledge of autism. Runs a school, at Struan Honor, and a residential community for autistic young people and adults, at Balmyre House. Information sheet and leaflet available, as well as National Autistic Society publications, such as *Children Apart*.

SCOTTISH SOCIETY FOR THE MENTALLY HANDICAPPED
13 Elmbank Street
Glasgow G2 4QA
Tel: 041-226-4541

Information, advice and support for families. Representation to government at all levels. Concerns include employment, residential care and recreational activities. Local groups. Publications, including journal *Newslink, Scots Law and The Mentally Handicapped* and *Information for the Named Person*.

SCOTTISH SPINA BIFIDA ASSOCIATION
190 Queensferry Road
Edinburgh EH4 2BW
Tel: 031-332-0743

Counselling, information, group and family holidays, sports training, independence workshops, leisure activities, family support. Local branches.

SCOTTISH SPINAL CORD INJURY ASSOCIATION
5 Shandwick Place
Edinburgh EH2 4RG
Tel: 031-228-3827

Information, advice, counselling and support for spinally injured people and
their families. Pressure group activities. Newsletter.

SCOTTISH SPORTS ASSOCIATION FOR THE DISABLED
Scottish Sports Council
1 St Colme Street
Edinburgh EH3 6AA
Tel: 031-225-8411

Promotes the development of sport and physical recreation for disabled people.

RNIB RESOURCE CENTRE FOR THE BLIND
276 St Vincent Street
Glasgow G3
Tel: 041-248-5811

Offers advice, information, and courses to students and staff on learning aids
and resources for the visually impaired.

SEND — SPECIAL EDUCATIONAL NEEDS DATABASE
Scottish Centre for Educational Technology
74 Victoria Crescent Road
Dowanhill
Glasgow G12 4JN
Tel: 041-334-9314

SEND is a viewdata base on the use of microelectronics for those with special
needs. Information sections include useful hardware, software, publications,
courses, conferences, exhibitions and contacts/sources of advice. SEND also
offers a MAILBOX and NOTICEBOARD facility and is available though
PRESTEL/page 515.

SENSE — THE NATIONAL DEAF-BLIND AND RUBELLA ASSOCIATION

311 Grays Inn Road   168 Dumbarton Road
London WC1X 8PT   Glasgow G11 6XE
Tel: 01-278-1005   Tel: 041-334-9666

Advice, information and support for families of deaf-blind children. Holiday
schemes. Self-help groups. Residential care conferences, training and research.
Journal *Talking Sense* and other publications, including *Out of Isolation:
introductory notes on the education of deaf-blind children* and *Information and
Awareness Pack*.

SEQUEL — SPECIAL EQUIPMENT AND AIDS FOR LIVING
Ddol Hir
Glyn Ceiriog
Llangollen
Clywd
Wales
Tel: 0691-72-331

Help and advice with the purchase of special electronic/electrical equipment
for severely disabled people. *Sequel Newsletter*.

SPECIAL EDUCATIONAL NEEDS NATIONAL ADVISORY COUNCIL
Hillside
271 Woolton Road
Liverpool L16 8NB
Tel: 051-722-3819

Information and promotion of policies in education for special needs.
Conferences. Leaflet *Developing the Curriculum for Children with Special
Educational Needs*.

TUBEROUS SCLEROSIS ASSOCIATION
Hon. Secretary   11 Deveron Road
Little Burnsley Farm   Glasgow G61 1LJ
Catshill   Tel: 041-942-6664
Bromsgrove
Worcestershire B61 0NQ
Tel: 0527-71898

Acts as a self-help group for parents and funds education and research;
promotes public understanding. Local meetings. Publications: fact sheets on
epilepsy, sleep problems, language, behaviour difficulties and other titles;
newsletter.

VOLUNTARY COUNCIL FOR HANDICAPPED CHILDREN
National Children's Bureau
8 Wakley Street
London EC1V 7QE
Tel: 01-278-9441

Offers information and support to parents and teachers of children with special
needs.

Official and professional bodies

Association of Directors of Education in Scotland	c/o Director of Education, Lothian Regional Council, 40 Torphichen Street, Edinburgh EH3 8JJ (Tel: 031-229-9166).
Commissioner for Local Administration in Scotland (Local Ombudsman)	5 Shandwick Place, Edinburgh EH2 4RG (Tel: 031-229-4472).
British Psychological Society	48 Princess Road East, Leicester LE1 7DR (Tel: 0533 549568 for current contact address of Scottish Division).
Committee on Special Educational Needs (COSPEN)	Scottish Consultative Council on the curriculum, New St. Andrew's House, Edinburgh EH1 2SX (Tel: 031-556-8400).
Convention of Scottish Local Authorities (COSLA)	Rosebery House, 9 Haymarket Terrace, Edinburgh EH12 5XZ (Tel: 031-346 1222).
Educational Institute of Scotland (EIS)	46 Moray Place, Edinburgh EH3 6BH (Tel: 031-225-6244).
Educational Publishers Council (EPC)	19 Bedford Square, London WC1 (Tel: 01-580-6321).
Houses of Parliament	Westminster, London SW1 (Tel: 01-219-3000).
Scottish Council for Educational Technology	74 Victoria Crescent Road, Glasgow G12 9JN (Tel: 041-334 9314).
Scottish Council for Research in Education	Moray House College, 15 St. John Street, Edinburgh EH8 8JR (Tel: 031-557-2944).
Scottish Educational Data Archive	Centre for Educational Sociology, University of Edinburgh, Buccleuch Place, Edinburgh 8 (Tel: 031-667-1011).
Scottish Education Department (SED) publications: (for Departmental Circulars) (for all other departmental publications not available from HMSO)	New St. Andrew's House, Edinburgh EH1 2SX (Tel: 031-556-8400). Room 323, 43 Jeffrey Street, Edinburgh EH 1DN Scottish Office Library, New St. Andrew's House.
Scottish Examination Board	Iron Mills Road, Dalkeith, Midlothian (Tel: 031-663-6601).
Scottish Information Office	New St. Andrew's House, Edinburgh EH1 3TD (Tel: 031-244-1111).

Scottish Secondary Teachers' Association	15 Dundas Street, Edinburgh EH3 6QG (Tel: 031-556-5919).
Scottish Vocational Education Council	38 Queen Street, Glasgow G1 3DY (Tel: 041-248-7900).

EDUCATION AUTHORITIES

Borders Regional Council	Director of Education, Education Department, Borders Regional Council, Regional Headquarters, Newtown St. Boswells TD6 0SA (Tel: 08352-3301).
Central Regional Council	Director of Education, Education Department, Central Regional Council, Regional Headquarters, Viewforth, Stirling FH8 2ET (Tel: 0786 3111).
Dumfries and Galloway Regional Council	Director of Education, Education Offices, Dumfries & Galloway Regional Council, 30 Edinburgh Road, Dumfries DG1 1JQ (Tel: 0387-63822).
Fife Regional Council	Director of Education, Education Department, Fife Regional Council, Regional Headquarters, Fife House, North Street, Glenrothes KY7 5LT (Tel: 0592-75411).
Grampian Regional Council	Director of Education, Education Department, Grampian Regional Council, Regional Headquarters, Woodhill House, Ashgrove Road West, Aberdeen (Tel: 0224 682222).
Highland Regional Council	Director of Education, Education Department, Highland Regional Council, Regional Building, Glenurquhart Road, Inverness IV3 5NX (Tel: 0463 34131).
Lothian Regional Council	Director of Education, Education Department, Lothian Regional Council, 40 Torphichen Street, Edinburgh EH3 8JJ (Tel: 031-229-9166).
Strathclyde Regional Council	Director of Education, Regional Education Office, Strathclyde Regional Council, 20 India Street, Glasgow G2 (Tel: 041-227-2847).
(Argyll Division)	Divisional Education Officer, Argyll Division, Argyll House, Alexandra Parade, Dunoon DA28 8AJ (Tel: 0369-4000).
(Ayr Division)	Divisional Education Officer, Ayr Division, Regional Offices, Ayr KA7 1DR (Tel: 0292-66922).
(Dumbarton Division)	Divisional Education Officer, Dumbarton Division, Regional Council Offices, Dumbarton G82 3PU (Tel: 0389-65151).
(Glasgow Division)	Divisional Education Officer, Glasgow Division, Education Offices, 129 Bath Street, Glasgow G2 4SY (Tel: 041-204-2900).
(Lanark Division)	Divisional Education Officer, Lanark Division, Regional Offices, Hamilton ML3 0AE (Tel: 0698-282828).

(Renfrew Division)	Divisional Education Officer, Renfrew Division, Regional Offices, Cotton Street, Paisley PA1 1LE (Tel: 041-889-5454).
Tayside Regional Council	Director of Education, Regional Education Office, Tayside Regional Council, Tayside House, 28 Crichton Street, Dundee DD1 3RJ (Tel: 0382-23281).
Orkney Islands Council	Director of Education, Education Department, Orkney Islands Council, Albert Street, Kirkwall KW15 1NY (Tel: 0856-3535).
Shetlands Islands Council	Director of Education, Education Offices, Shetlands Islands Council, 1 Harbour Street, Lerwick ZE1 0LS (Tel: 0595-3535).
Western Isles Islands Council	Director of Education, Education Office, Western Isles Council, Sandwick Road, Stornoway, Lewis PA87 2BW .

Key Terms explained*

Adaptations

Altering equipment, buildings or furnishings to facilitate use by people who would otherwise have difficulty in using these (for example, widening doors for wheelchair users, designing desks which prevent books sliding off, provision of tools or machines that can be operated without both hands).

Appeals

Parents or (with certain exceptions) young persons who disagree with a decision to open a Record of Needs or not or with statements in certain parts of the Record can try to get things changed by appealing. Their appeal is first considered by an appeal committee, which must refer the case to the Secretary of State for a decision about a recording matter (but not about ordinary choice of school appeals not involving a recording matter). The appeal committee decides whether or not a parent's choice of school should be granted, but it must do so in accordance with any decision by the Secretary of State, as must the sheriff court in dealing with any choice of school appeals connected with a recording decision.

Aptitude

Usually refers to capability in a particular skill, such as drawing, playing a musical instrument, conducting a scientific experiment, creative writing and so on.

Ascertainment

The term previously used to denote the selection of children for special education before this was taken over by the recording process under the Education (Scotland) Act 1981.

Assessment

The process of finding out what a child's special educational needs are and how they should be catered for. It may span over a period of weeks or even months, depending on a child's difficulties, involving observations and discussions as well as formal examinations. The assessment may be initiated at a very early age, perhaps well before a child starts school, but assessments can be carried out at a much later age as well. The assessment will include a medical assessment and probably a formal medical examination, psychological assessments, educational and possibly social worker's reports; parents are also expected to be involved. Parents are entitled to ask for an assessment without waiting for the education authority to initiate one. The assessment may or may not result in the drawing up of a Record of Needs, depending on the nature of the child's difficulties.

---

*Cross references are in *italics*.

Assessment profile

Part of the Record of Needs which says what the child's strengths and weaknesses are. It should be written in plain language.

Attainment/achievement

How well pupils do in various educational activities, often shown by grades or marks for classwork, in tests, exams, and so on. Children may "over" or "underachieve" if they do better or worse than expected.

Auxiliary or ancillary help

Help for pupils in difficulty with practical tasks such as changing, feeding, operating equipment, toileting and so on. Non-teaching staff may be appointed to provide this auxiliary help. Schools may also use auxiliary staff for setting up equipment for classroom use, dispensing materials and so on.

Choice of school

Parents and *young persons* have a legal right to ask the education authority for their own choice of school, by making a *placing request* and *appealing* if necessary. The authority may only turn down a request if certain legally defined grounds apply, such as the authority having to spend an unreasonable amount of money to offer a place there. Parents can ask a choice of ordinary rather than *special school*, or vice versa, but in any case where the nature and extent of special educational need is at issue the matter may have to be referred, on appeal, to the *Secretary of State* before the appeal committee can decide whether the parent's choice of school should be upheld.

Complex special educational needs

Special educational needs arising from a number of difficulties — not all of them necessarily severe — in such areas as behaviour, learning, mobility, speech, and so on.

Conductive education

An approach to education, pioneered in Hungary, for children with cerebral palsy and spina bifida, who are taught through combined music, movement and other exercises to acquire independence skills in preparation for entry into ordinary schools.

Counselling/guidance

Providing social support for children and young people or their parents in difficulties, helping them to understand and cope with their difficulties, and perhaps pointing to practical solutions to help come to terms or overcome them. Counselling is likely to take the form of listening, discussion, offering encouragement, role play, making assessments and so on, probably with a view to getting the person to work out for themselves the most appropriate action. In secondary schools, teachers of guidance are specially appointed to advise pupils and their parents about curriculum, personal and vocational matters.

Additional or specialist counselling may be provided for pupils with special educational needs by other staff within or outwith the school.

Curriculum

The areas of study or range of subjects taught at school or other educational establishment. The law does not say what should be taught at school, but the education provided should be according to the age, ability and aptitude of the child and any special educational needs he or she has. The areas of study which are normally compulsory, such as language, arts and mathematics, are referreed to as the "core curriculum". From the third year of secondary school, pupils will ususally be given some choice over what they wish to study, both within and outwith the core curriculum. Pupils with particular learning difficulties may follow a modified curriculum suited to their pace or method of learning.

Disability

A condition (mental, physical, sensory, etc.) giving rise to difficulty or inability in performing some task, acquiring some skill or understanding something. The difficulty may also reflect to some extent the expectations people place on others to perform to certain standards. The disability may also be relative to the way people are taught, what they are taught, or the support they are given.

Discontinuance of Record

The *Record of Needs* may be discontinued as a result of an appeal, review decision or a parent or young person asking for the Record to be discontinued upon reaching school leaving age. It is automatically discontinued once age 18 is reached. The discontinued record will be preserved for another 5 years, unless the parent or young person asks for it to be destroyed.

Examination (medical)

Children undergoing *assessment* (including medical assessment) for special educational needs are also likely to receive a formal medical examination. Parents are entitled to be present at the medical examination. The examination will help those assessing the child to identify any physical or other *impairments* which might affect learning. In addition, education authorities, through the school health service, will arrange for pupils to receive routine medical checks on starting or transferring school and at other times. Parents risk breaking the law for refusing or failing to let their child be medically examined. The school must normally have its own medical room and have arrangements for giving first aid.

Examinations (school)

Arrangements are normally made for pupils to be examined in different school activities or subjects, mainly through written answers to exam papers but through oral and practical work as well. Schools may arrange their own internal exams but will present pupils for external public exams as well, such as the Scottish Certificate of Education, normally taken in the fourth to sixth years of secondary school. Special arrangements may be made for pupils with special educational needs to sit examinations, such as provision of extra time, special equipment, materials or other practical help for giving answers.

Future needs assessment

The process of finding out what future provision should be made for a recorded pupil (aged 14-15^1/4) after reaching school leaving age at 16, including whether or not he or she should continue to be recorded. Parents are entitled to their own copy of the report on their child's future needs assessment. The assessment should be linked to one carried out by the social work department, if the pupil is disabled, to work out his or her welfare requirements in relation to other social services.

Handicap

A condition which in given circumstances leaves a person at a disadvantage, economically, educationally, socially or in some other sense. The condition itself need not be the cause of the handicap, which may be more a reflection of negative attitudes and restrictive opportunities placed before people with certain difficulties. The categories of "handicap" in which children with special needs were placed were abolished in 1981. Nowadays the term 'handicap', with its connotation of personal inadequacy, tends to be avoided in education.

Hospital schooling

Children and young people who need constant medical care and attention may have to attend a hospital school in order to continue with their education. Length of stay will obviously depend on the child's medical or physical condition, possibly lasting throughout schooling in the severest cases, but the authority may arrange for pupils to spend some of their time at ordinary school. Arrangements may be made for children with short-term illness or injuries or who are having an operation to receive education from resident or visiting teachers during their stay in hospital.

Impairment

Difficulty in hearing, moving, speaking, understanding and so on. Impairments may vary from severe, such as not being able to see or hear at all, to mild or moderate, such as partial sight or hearing. Impairments may also be general, such as difficulty in moving about at all, or specific, such as difficulty in moving or controlling certain parts of the body only.

Intelligence/intelligence tests

There are many varied and conflicting views about what "intelligence" is, one view being that intelligence is simply what intelligence tests measure! Most intelligence tests deal with reasoning, memory, numerical and other abilities, to give a person's intelligence quotient (IQ). Most experts are agreed that intelligence is affected by environmental factors, such as stimulus and support from the home and how and what children are taught at school, but biological factors may have some influence as well.

Integration

A generic term for the education of children with special needs alongside children in ordinary school. Integration may take different forms: educating children with special needs in ordinary schools but in separate classes or units some or all of the time; education in the same classes as other children but possibly following a different or modified curriculum; following the same school curriculum as other children in the class but backed up with specialist tuition or other support.

Learning difficulty

A difficulty ranging from difficulty in learning anything at all to less severe difficulties or specific difficulties in learning, for example, in developing certain skills, such as reading or in coping with ideas or concepts. Learning difficulties may also be related to other difficulties, arising from say, an emotional problem or frequent absence from school. Physical disabilities or impairments need not in themselves give rise to learning difficulties except if suitable support is not provided (e.g. specialist instruction, special aids to learning).

Named Person

The person appointed by the education authority to whom parents and young people with a Record of Need can turn to for advice and information, for example, in deciding whether to *appeal*. The Named Person is appointed at the time the *Record of Needs* is opened. This should be somebody, such as a friend or professional worker, who is acceptable to the parent or young person, who may however opt not to have a Named Person. The Named Person should not be confused with the official appointed to offer advice and information earlier on, at the time of *assessment*.

Parent

The parent, under the Education (Scotland) Act 1980, includes a guardian or any other person liable to maintain or having actual custody of a child or young person. Both parents are normally responsible for making sure that their child is properly educated, usually by seeing that their child attends school regularly. Where parents are separated or divorced and there is a court order for custody of the child, legal responsibility rests with the parent given custody. If there is no court order for custody, both parents continue to be responsible, even if they are living apart. If the child is in care, parents may share responsibility with the child's foster parent or whoever is in charge.

Placing request

A written request to the education authority by parents naming the school(s), in order of preference, they would like their child to attend, if different from the school proposed by the authority. A placing request can be made at any time, but normally it will be made before the child is due to start or transfer school. Placing requests can be refused on certain legally prescribed grounds, but parents (and young persons) can appeal against a refusal, although they can only appeal once in every 12 months.

Portage

A system developed in the United States, in which parents and professional staff work closely together to further the development of children with special needs, such as both partners sharing "expertise" in helping children to learn to read or other educational tasks.

Progress record

A document/file kept by the education authority containing information about each pupil's progress in schoolwork, school attendance, medical condition, home background and other details. Progress records need not be shown to parents but the education authority may nonetheless agree to them being shown. The law may soon be changed to allow parents to see their child's school records, however. The progress record should not be confused with the *Record of Need* or with *school reports* sent to parents.

Pronounced special educational needs

Special educational needs arising from difficulties which are severe in one or more areas, such as hearing, learning, speech, and so on.

Psychological service

Formerly known as the 'child guidance service', the psychological service forms part of the education authority concerned with the assessment and recording of children with special educational needs and with children having other difficulties with schooling.

Recording

The process of drawing up a Record of Needs. Parents will be shown a draft of the Record and invited to give their own comments before it is finalised.

Record of Needs

An official document drawn up by the education authority giving details of what a child's special educational needs are and how these should be catered for. The Record also includes space for parent's comments and other details. A copy of this document must be given to every parent of a 'recorded' child. Parents can appeal against a decision to record or not and against certain parts of the record.

Remedial education/teaching

Conventionally refers to help within an ordinary school for pupils who are making slow progress in activities like learning to read or number work, with these pupils often working in smaller groups or being taught individually outwith normal class for these activities. The Warnock committee believed that the term remedial education was no longer a useful one and suggested it be dropped in favour of education for children with learning difficulties, covering children in special and ordinary schools.

Responsible party

The parent, guardian, young person or whoever is legally responsible for the person for whom the Record of Needs has been opened. The responsible party is invited to comment on the draft Record of Needs, in the space provided, before it is finalised.

Reviews

The process of considering whether a child should continue to be recorded or not and whether the information in the Record needs to be changed or brought up to date. Children have to be re-assessed before any review decisions can be reached. Parents can appeal against review decisions.

School report

A document normally issued to parents at least once a year saying how their child is progressing in school work at school, remarking on their conduct and drawing attention to any difficulties their child is having. Schools may arrange for parents to comment on or discuss their child's school report with staff.

Secretary of State

A cabinet minister in overall charge of a central government department. The Secretary of State for Scotland is concerned with Scottish affairs, including education, although a junior non-cabinet minister is usually appointed to deal with Scottish education as well. Appeals against a recording decision are referred to the Secretary of State's advisers.

Sheriff court

The sheriff court can be appealed to by parents or young persons where request on their own *choice of school* has been turned down by an *appeal* committee. The sheriff must have regard to any decision by the Secretary of State if the appeal is linked to a recording decision (or refer the case to the Secretary of State for specialist advice if this has not already been done).

Special educational needs

Children are said to have special educational needs if they have significantly greater difficulties in learning compared with the majority of children of their age or if they have a disability which prevents them from taking proper advantage of education in the ordinary way. A *Record of Needs* must be opened for these children if their special educational needs are *pronounced, specific* or *complex* and are such as to require 'continuing review'.

Specific special educational needs

Special educational needs arising from a limited and usually well-defined difficulty, such as dyslexia.

Special School/class

A school/class catering wholly or mainly for pupils with a Record of Needs. Most are run by education authorities, but a number of them are by voluntary organisations, such as schools for blind or deaf children and for children with cerebral palsy. Some special schools are residential.

Statement of Needs

The equivalent document in England and Wales to the *Record of Needs*

In Scotland, the "statement of special educational needs" is the part of the Record of Needs describing in detail what the child's special educational needs are and what measures are required to deal with them effectively. Parents can appeal against the statement.

Summary of impairments

Part of the Record of Needs identifying the causes of the child's difficulties and the sort of specialist help required.

Therapy

Helping people to adjust or adapt to some impairment, carry out particular tasks or develop certain skills which present difficulties, and generally learn to cope with everyday demands. Therapy may include physical exercise, skills training, learning to use special aids and equipment, counselling, and so on.

Young person

A person who has reached school leaving age (age 16 approx.) but who is not yet 18. Young persons at school assume the legal rights of their parents over matters like asking for an *assessment*, choice of school *appeals*, appealing against a *recording* decision, or turning to a *Named Person* for advice and information. In certain circumstances, however, the parent may continue to exercise these rights if the young person is deemed incapable of expressing his or her wishes.

Warnock report

The report of the commmittee set up by the government to enquire into and make recommendations about the education of children and young people with special educational needs. The report was published in 1978. See reading list for further details.

Index

Note the abbreviation SEN has been used for special educational needs.

Printed in Scotland for HMSO by (56901)
Dd. 0287198 ① HF4744 C40 1/89